Love is the brightest STAR that leads

'Can we cover the earth with leather so it's
soft wherever we go? No . . . so what can we
do? We can wear leather sandals. It is equal
to covering the earth with leather.

'Likewise, enemies are as limitless as
space. All enemies cannot possibly be overcome. Yet if one can just overcome hatred,
this will be equal to overcoming all enemies.
All that is unsatisfactory in the world, all the
fear and suffering that exists, clinging to the
'I' has created it. What am I to do with this
great demon? To release myself from harm
and free all others from their suffering, let
me give myself away and love others as I
love myself. If a problem can be solved, why
be unhappy? And if a problem cannot be
solved, what is the use of being unhappy?'

From *The Cup*, a film by Khyentse Norbu

Green Tara* holds a prominent position in
the cultures of Tibet and Nepal. The name
Tara means 'She who liberates'.
*see girlossary for full reference

First published in 2001

Allen & Unwin
83 Alexander St
Crows Nest NSW 2065
Australia
Phone: (61 2) 8425 0100
Fax: (61 2) 9906 2218
Email: info@allenandunwin.com
Web: www.allenandunwin.com

National Library of Australia
Cataloguing-in-Publication entry:

Paul, Anthea.
      Girlosophy 2: the love survival kit.

      ISBN 1 86508 585 5.

      1.Young women – Life skills guides. 2.Self-perception in women.
      3. Women and spiritualism. 4. Love. I. Title.

177.7

Concept and art direction by Anthea Paul
Design by Justine O'Donnell
Photography by Ashley de Prazer, Marcus Clinton and Lawrence Dowd
Edited by Jude McGee
Girlosophy 2 CD produced by Tom Middleton, London, UK
Legal counsel: Allen Allen & Hemsley, Sydney, Australia
Website: www.girlosophy.com by The Revolution

'Is This Love?' written by Bob Marley. Lyric reprint courtesy of the Marley
Estate. Publishers – Bob Marley Music/Rykomusic Ltd/Festival Music Pty Ltd.

Printed in China by Everbest Printing Co. Ltd

10 9 8 7 6 5 4 3 2 1

girlosophy ②

THE
LOVE
SURVIVAL KIT

anthea paul

ALLEN&UNWIN

contents

Introduction

Welcome to *The Love Survival Kit*! Once again I am writing to pass on a few of the lessons I've learnt on this long and winding, endlessly fascinating, occasionally terrifying, mostly hilarious, always moving, ever brilliant and sometimes tragic road of life.

Why *The Love Survival Kit*? Well, why not? Love is the source of all creation so we should give it close examination at every stage of our lives. Love is a mystery at some point for all of us, and those who write about it typically declare their inadequacy for the task. But I believe we are all equally well resourced to speak or write about love, so long as we get back to our true essence – pure love.

These days, there is much emphasis on romantic love, but this is usually just a temporary fantasy designed to get you started on the real process of loving. The point of *The Love Survival Kit* is to show the wider meaning of love as a tool, as a resource and as a force.

What I have hoped to do in this book is look at love in the broadest sense. Love is a force that helps you overcome all that is negative. It allows each of us the chance to effect great changes in our lives, on a moment-by-moment basis. And as love changes our lives so too does it touch others. Love is not an isolated thing but an energy that permeates and penetrates.

It is often said that only love is real and all else is illusion. One thing that I have concluded is that whatever you do – any activity at all – and whomever you do it with or to, you are actually only doing one of two things: you are either showing or not showing love. As the saying goes, love is as love does. So you see, love's got everything to do with it.

Love itself is therefore the ultimate survivor in the game of life and the true survivor's trump card is to *become* love, to actually *be* love. Love is pure consciousness and this is made manifest by being at one with the energy of the Universe. When you are this in flow you see and understand all things as being one, and all things are possible.

As I understand it, getting to grips with this mighty truth is the number one task we have been sent to do. It's why we've arrived on the earthly plane in human form. And we had all better get with the

Love is not only the essence of creation, but also the essence of soul survival. Love is the messenger of the soul and we are all receivers and transmitters. The  frequency and the content is up to each of us as individuals in alignment with our destiny, for love is there to fulfil your soul's journey and light the way for others at the same time.

program, for we ignore it at our peril. But it's no longer just about each one of us, although we must take personal responsibility for ourselves. Now it has to be about all of us, everything in existence, and our responsibility to those whom we don't know and may never know, now or in the future. We must overextend ourselves in love by any means necessary. We need love for our very survival – to give and also to receive it in all its forms. We need to understand and most of all practice the small acts of love that lead to acceptance of all races and all species, which is the only way to achieve greater harmony within ourselves and the environment. Otherwise, we won't survive as humans, let alone as a planet.

With maturity, time and the eventual exhaustion of our desires in the physical world, it becomes patently obvious that the only thing we take with us is the love we generated while we were here. Money alone doesn't make the trip worth it. Not even partially. Mahatma Gandhi reportedly died with about two dollars to his name. But he left a legacy of love and was passionately revered by hundreds of millions of people. His Holiness, The Dalai Lama of Tibet, is another who spends his earthly days leading by example through practicing his own exquisite form of compassion and love.

The Love Survival Kit is therefore essential – a resource kit for your journey, your personal grab-bag for all the situations that life can, and will, throw up. It will be there for you in any emergency and will hopefully show you time and time again the different types of love, as well as the power of faith, which holds it all together.

The subjects in the photographs are people from all walks of life and often from different parts of the world. In some cases they have made long journeys in the name of love. They are brothers and sisters, mothers and daughters, boyfriends and girlfriends, friends and life companions of different ages and nationalities. They are real people. I feel we should celebrate that, no matter where we come from, we are all different and yet so very similar. For the most part we all want the same thing: to love and to be loved.

As well as showing their beauty of spirit, the *girlosophy*[2] girls, boys, men and women all showed me much love by their generous participation and I am very grateful for their support and for their trust. Their enthusiasm and love of life kept me going, spurring me to try even harder. I hope I can return that love and justify their faith in me with the completion of this book.

My own life/love (love life!) odyssey has been chock-full of twists and turns, containing many wonderful (and some not-so-wonderful) surprises. While writing this book it was more than instructive to note the circumstances where I had failed to be loving or where I hadn't succeeded in loving. At times this was heartbreaking to contemplate but it also served to enable me to punch a mental fist in the air when I had succeeded (happily, more and more frequently).

This book follows on from *A Soul Survival Kit*. They are not the same, yet they are intimately connected, because love is the food of the soul and the soul is love's ultimate home and destination. The seven chapters of *The Love Survival Kit* are based on the seven chakras, reflecting the process that we each need to undergo in order to realize our own – and love's – potential.

Love is not only the essence of creation but also the essence of soul survival. Love is the messenger of the soul and we are all receivers and transmitters. The frequency and the content is up to each of us as individuals in alignment with our destiny, for love is there to fulfil your soul's journey and light the way for others at the same time.

I have tried to make the book a cornucopia of positive ideas, images and design so that it can serve as both an inspiration and a meditation. The more that you meditate, concentrate or focus on something, the more it becomes a reality in your life. As Ernest Holmes said, 'Where the mind goes, energy flows'. What could be better, then, than to focus on love? What more joy could there possibly be than to make your first response and your primary motivation in life one of love? If you want love, then you need to think about it, show it, reflect upon it, embody it and give it. Heaps. In other words, if you want to reach your full potential as a human it's got to be 'Access All Areas'. With love as your guide you can achieve anything that you want.

So get ready to pack up and hit the road in your own version of the Love Bus. Above all follow your heart – there's a whole Universe waiting to be explored …

Anthea Paul

What's in your love survival kit?
Here's what's in girlosophy's:

map: a guide to the songlines and landscape of your personal heartland
compass: to help you stay faithfully on course when the darkness sets in
bandages: to heal and bind the many superficial wounds inflicted by the journey
pocket knife: to cut away the branches that occasionally block the path and to cut the cords of the past so you keep moving forward
matches: to light your own fire and hold the candle that's yours alone to hold
food: optimal sustenance for the right energy on your journey
water: pure filtered life force for total cleansing on all levels
protection: your personal barriers and support network so you don't become faded, tired and brittle from exposure to the elements
disinfectant: your detox routine to keep infections from setting in after minor scrapes
tape, needle and thread: to mend where you can so you don't have to throw things out unnecessarily
photos: of those who mean something to you and to remind you that you are loved in return

SPIRIT

UNDAUNTED

REALITY

VOW

INNER STRENGTH

VICTORY

AFFIRMATION

LOVE

survival

spirit
undaunted
eality
ow
integrated
victory
affirms
life

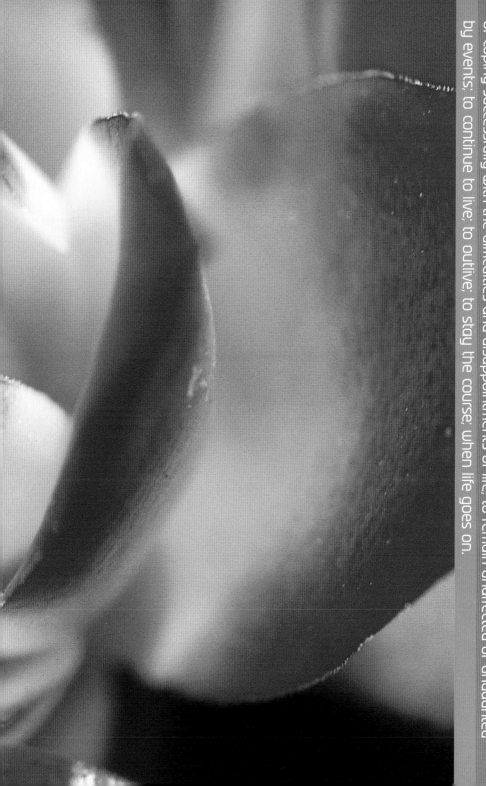

CHAKRA: base or root chakra: Center for the individual being linked with the world in physical form; the basis for self-expression and ambition, tempered by the desire to evolve, protect self and survive

[defn] To remain alive or exist after the cessation of something or the occurrence of some event; the act of coping successfully with the difficulties and disappointments of life; to remain unaffected or undaunted by events; to continue to live; to outlive; to stay the course; when life goes on.

It's survival of the fittest,
especially in matters of the heart.
Have you been training?

'BEING SINGLE IS BEST, BUT
EVERYONE WANTS TO FALL IN LOVE.'

Andy Warhol, *Love, Love, Love*

Sole survival — the mystery of intimacy

Survival is the ground level of existence and everyone has to transcend it before they can fully bond and love another person unconditionally. Yet everyone is confused some of the time if not all of the time about love. Because love is mysterious and that's the point: it appears and it vanishes.

Every time we connect with someone we have an opportunity to grow, by learning to love or at least to demonstrate that we'd like to try. Growth comes through relationships with your parents, friends, an intimate partner, God – but especially with yourself. Your relationship with yourself is the one relationship that truly is long term, the one that survives until the end, and it's the most intimate relationship you will ever have.

So if you are single, either consciously or by default, or perhaps beginning a new phase or relationship in your life, use the time wisely to learn the hidden parts of yourself that may be the key to understanding who you really are. Spend time or live alone for a while, and learn to look after yourself. Use the opportunity to prepare for the future.

We all dream about finding a love with one partner that is lasting. It is possible to have it – you just need to believe that it is. But intimacy with another person starts with you and your intimate relationship with yourself. So it may be you that's the mystery – not love!

Love, rather than another person, completes us. And the role of lasting love in our lives reveals our highest potential to ourselves and the world.

Like plants we need to be free to reach the light and the rain — love and awareness — in order to grow

To be successful in your life and in love – your life and your love life are one and the same thing – you need to get past feelings of insecurity stemming from fears of loneliness, rejection or abandonment. Don't give in to those feelings: they'll hold you back and undermine your courage and integrity when you need them the most.

That's the only difference between success and perceived failure – the courage and strength to be natural and real. Have a go.

'WHEN TWO PATHS OPEN UP YOU SHOULD ALWAYS

YOU SHOULD ALWAYS

From *Himalaya*, a film by Eric Valli

BEFORE YOU,
CHOOSE THE HARDEST ONE.'

At the start of a new relationship it all comes easily. That's why it's the start: the Universe breaks you in gently. All beginnings are gentle, but especially the beginnings of love, because love is the most important lesson and the Universe wants you to succeed.

But just because it's easy at the start, don't expect it to stay that way. The Universe will begin to load you up with harder lessons and tests to give you a real understanding of the long-term process that is love. You'll find that continuing to love someone in the same way that you did at the beginning of the relationship is impossible. Instead, allow each moment to have its corresponding 'love' equivalent. Each moment is as unique as each love.

Now you are on a steep love-learning curve. Loving seems to get harder and harder. Eventually, though, it will start to get easier. Love is designed this way because we are all here to learn how to love. We start off with our families, and our platonic intimates then move on to our romantic and sexual partners. The ultimate love test is to extend our love to every person and being in existence. The great masters of love have reached this level.

BELONG TO YOURSELF. THEN AND ONLY THEN CAN YOU PROPERLY GIVE YOURSELF TO SOMEONE ELSE.

Love fitness quiz

When you're assessing the relationship potential of a person, it helps to check out their overall circumstances.

How's their mentality? Are they happy, depressed, satisfied or dissatisfied with their life? What's their lifestyle? Are they healthy or not; do they go out frequently or stay home; do they drink too much or take drugs? What's their family life or background? Did they have a traumatic or stable childhood; do their parents get along well; are they in regular contact with their family?

It's important to get a sense of the kinds of obligations they have, including family, career, sport or hobbies, as well as some idea of their life in general. Are they stable at home and in their job, or are they about to be evicted or fired? Have they previously or recently been through a traumatic experience (like the death of a parent, or a serious car accident)? Are they having cash flow hassles?

All these things may have an impact on you. If things aren't going well for them, starting a relationship will probably be a low priority.

So get the full picture before you make them your priority. Ask yourself the hard questions. And don't take them on as some kind of cause, either. Because it's their stuff, not yours.

Take care
When you have something
— a pet, a home, your
body, a car, a relationship
— you have to maintain it.
It's your responsibility.

13

Respect your body

Life is not about having approval for what you look like, what labels you wear, or what gig you may have going. It's not about what others say is groovy or IN. It's about YOU and being who YOU are. Dance to your own beat. Stay healthy: exercise, eat good food, breathe fresh air and drink plenty of water. Do it for yourself, not for anyone else. And then when you do meet someone who rocks your world, you won't panic and rush into a crazy diet and gym schedule.

You've only got one

love the icon within

ICON LOVE:

it's the flavor of the new millennium. Madonna, Princess Diana, Michael Jordan, Julia Roberts, Brad Pitt – the names are as familiar to us as our own, as are the life stories that go with each. But why do we put so much love into celebrities, strangers most of us have never met but about whom we know so much? We applaud people who have dared to follow their destiny. We respect those who appear to have a strong sense of self, whatever the reality may be. We trust and put faith in people whose desires have been so strongly manifested and whose belief in themselves seems to be unshakeable. But ultimately we adore and worship those who appear to have transcended themselves – we see this as a magical thing. Often we revere them because they are physically ideal to us in some way. (And this is where we get seriously off-track. Because their beauty is unique to them, just as we all have our own beauty, unique to each of us.) We single them out and reserve for them a special place, as special people. While some celebrities may be all of these things, many are not. We devote too much energy to loving icons when we should be seeking and following our own destiny. By comparing their beauty to our own we are projecting energy onto them and away from ourselves. Living through others is a recipe for regret. If our icons can find the essence in themselves and bring it out to show the world, we can too. For we are as special as any celebrity. We are each uniquely gifted and the only thing separating us from those we idolize is our own lack of vision for ourselves. WE ARE ALL SUPERSTARS. So light your own candle for the future and love the icon within first.

Be a Life Adventurer

When someone leaves you, it's easy to feel that you did something wrong or said something to make it happen. That what happened was all your fault. You can feel that way, and take up the flag of The Victim. Or you can decide that it was part of the grand plan set out especially for you by the Universe to move you on to the next stage of your adventure. Carry the flag of The Life Adventurer instead! Remember that you're here to chalk up as many experiences along the way as are necessary to help you to uncover and discover your personal destiny.

hurt = temporary pain

damage = long-term hurt + long-term pain

Avoid damage: deal with your hurt when it first crops up.

'Everything moves, nothing stays,
and I should not hold on.'

| Ilse Bing, photographer and poet

Breaking-up...The soft landing

When you break up with someone you need a strategy to cope with the separation and to recover. It doesn't matter whether you were the person who made the decision to leave or whether it was your ex's decision.

There are a few simple rules to getting over a break-up:

CLOSURE: Hear or break the news, take or give some time apart, forgive or mend past wrongs, communicate the pain or regret. Do all these things as calmly as possible.

CLEAN: Toss out junk. Vacuum. Mop. Clean. It's amazingly therapeutic and it will keep you busy for a while. You'll have a sense of achievement when you're finished.

STORAGE: Put reminders away! Pinboards, photo frames, items of clothing, certain CDs, any gifts – whatever it is, if it reminds you of the past get rid of it or put it into storage. The rule is: look at the object and ask, 'Energy up or energy down?'

TIME OUT: What are you waiting for? Now is the perfect time to use those Frequent Flyer points and annual leave. Go somewhere fabulous and leave the past behind for real. The postcards you can send are worth it! If you can't possibly get away for a long trip, take a day off work or school and have a long weekend.

FRESH START: It's a good time to plan the new phase of your life and devote time to yourself. Review all areas and map out exactly what it is you really want.

HEALTH AND FITNESS: This is the part where you really need to get with the program. Physical activity is a proven antidepressant and the endorphin charge is a natural high. Get into it and get over it – fast.

NEW FRIENDS: You can't stay at home and mope forever. Get out there and meet new people. Even if you feel terrible it's important to make new friends, and you never know who they know.

NEW ACTIVITIES: There's a world waiting to be discovered. The old cliché works: join the club, sign up for the course. Just do it.

The [Girlo]

Way of the Samurai

Love protects us. Use love to wrap yourself in and you can be a warrior in all areas of your life. Love has always been. Be yourself, be love and be a survivor.

SOMETIMES IT'S A RELIEF TO

If someone tells you that you're too good for them, they are really telling you they don't feel worthy. Sometimes it's a good idea to listen. There might be something in it. Because if they can't love themselves, they may not be able to love you either.

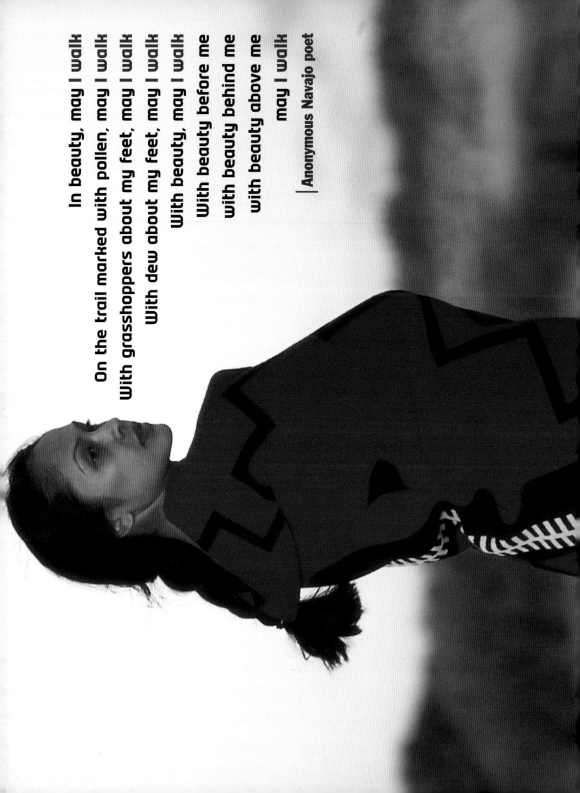

In beauty, may I walk
On the trail marked with pollen, may I walk
With grasshoppers about my feet, may I walk
With dew about my feet, may I walk
With beauty, may I walk
With beauty before me
with beauty behind me
with beauty above me
may I walk

—Anonymous Navajo poet

As one **takes off**

...another
one
lands.

sexuality

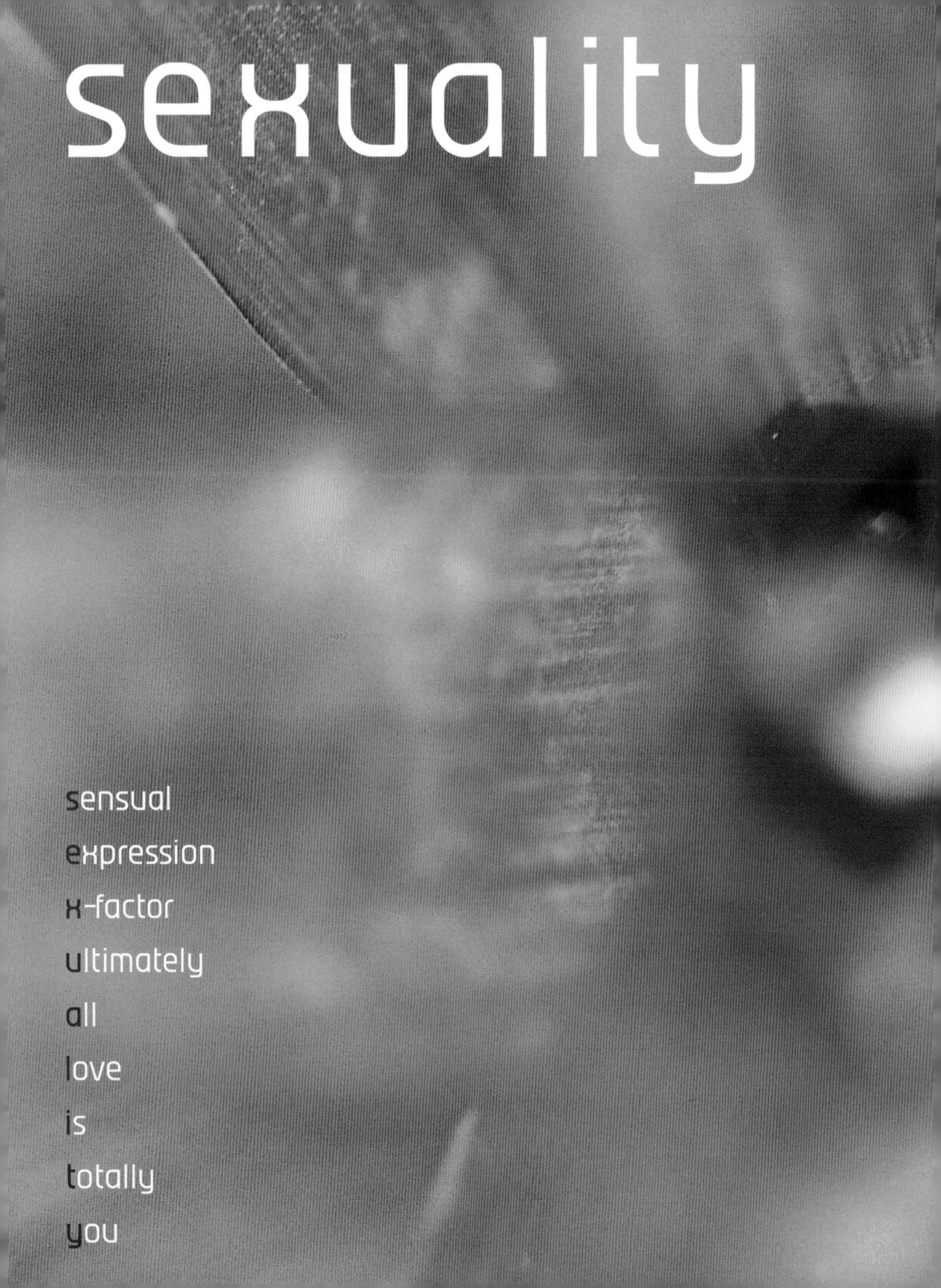

sensual

expression

x-factor

ultimately

all

love

is

totally

you

CHAKRA. **lower abdomen chakra**. Center of sexuality, all relationships and creativity

[def:n] Sexual nature and character of each individual; the recognition and emphasis of sexual matters; that which defines and drives individuals to behave in a particular way; the ideas and belief systems having to do with sexual relationships and sex.

Gorgeous

What's
not to
love?

BE THE ULTIMATE DANCING PARTNER

Step lightly
Smile confidently
Tread warily
Move gracefully
Bend softly
Lift reverently
Observe carefully
Follow knowingly
Dip thoughtfully
Fall gently
Hold regularly
Merge willingly
Swap occasionally
Shift rhythmically
Twist brilliantly
Sway intuitively
Hesitate rarely
Connect beautifully
Release frequently
Understand perfectly

Sex is a form of communication, so use it as a means of expression with someone who can understand it. Taking on intimate casual partners is, in Universal law, taking on their karmic energies, which is all the more reason to be selective. Don't just open up to anybody; you need to choose carefully who is worthy. It's an EXCHANGE OF ENERGY. Make it worthwhile. And remember, the art of love is far greater than the act

YOUR NATURAL
STATE IS PURE
AND IT MUST BE
PROTECTED. AS
IT IS WITH
NATURE, SO IT
IS WITH YOU.

The art of love

(Don't) Just do it

The time to be physically intimate with someone is a question of individual readiness. Some people feel comfortable enough to express themselves physically soon after meeting someone. Others need to wait longer before moving to this level. There is no blanket formula for the timing, so whether it's the third or the twentieth date, it should happen only when it feels right. It should never feel like pressure. The heart takes time to sort through the impulses of desire – which is not to say it can't grow in tandem, but if you really want to be sure of the heart's engagement, you should definitely wait.

Safety first

If you're old enough to have sex, you're old enough to take responsibility for your health and that of your partner. There are no shortcuts to safe sex – you have to protect yourself, and that means insisting on using a condom. You must use a condom and that's all there is to it.

Sexually transmitted diseases don't listen to excuses. HIV does not discriminate or show up looking like a certain type of person. And there's no desire in the world that can't survive the wait for a trip to the corner store if necessary.

Care for your friends, too. If it appears they may be going to have sex with someone, check that they have protection and help them to find or buy it if they don't.

Safe I is I as I safe I does.

...love by the way you walk, the

|Thich Nhat Hanh, Zen Buddhist Master

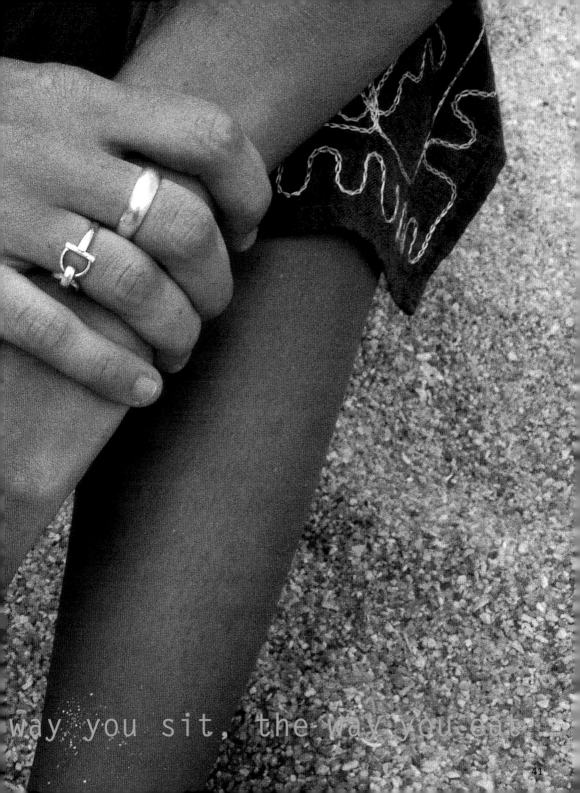

way you sit, the way you eat...

Free will is a treasure.
How much you exercise it reflects how much you love yourself.

Sleep alone from time to time.

Love sport

There are as many types of relationships as there are athletic events. Which event are you in? Are you lining up for a 100-meter sprint or setting out on a marathon? The marathon is epic and requires endurance, and all who enter are rewarded in some way. But there can be as much glory in a sprint, where mutual energy is expended over a short course and everyone knows their place at the end.

Go for the burn

Slow-burning love affairs sometimes bring the most satisfaction. Affairs that are all fireworks in the beginning, fiercely driven by the passion that goes with intense attraction, are often the ones that explode. So go easy. Stay light. Slow and smouldering works.

Action man...

You can't always tell what a person is like purely by what they say. Actions count for lots more. Look at how they walk, move and talk. Where's the softness, what's the real vibe? Are they humane with animals, gentle with young children, patient with other people? Do they have respect — for the environment, for others, FOR YOU, for themselves? Actions are beyond excuses. If they want to do the right thing, they will, and that's the only evidence you need.

Get close.

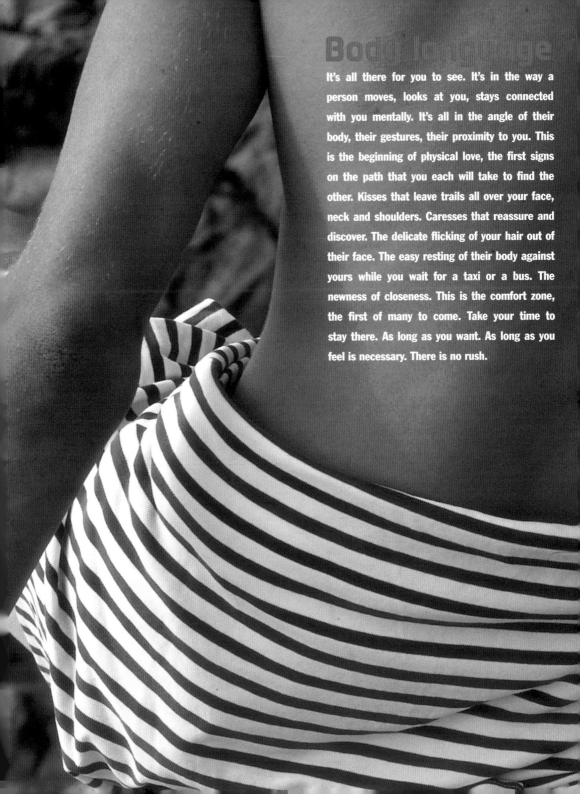

Body language

It's all there for you to see. It's in the way a person moves, looks at you, stays connected with you mentally. It's all in the angle of their body, their gestures, their proximity to you. This is the beginning of physical love, the first signs on the path that you each will take to find the other. Kisses that leave trails all over your face, neck and shoulders. Caresses that reassure and discover. The delicate flicking of your hair out of their face. The easy resting of their body against yours while you wait for a taxi or a bus. The newness of closeness. This is the comfort zone, the first of many to come. Take your time to stay there. As long as you want. As long as you feel is necessary. There is no rush.

When you are

in love

with life,

nothing is too hard. Everything
has freshness and reason.
And all is as it is.

Our most powerful drive is the sex drive.

Because sexual energy is not just energy that is applied to the physical expression of love. It is a potent energy source that can be applied to all endeavors. It can take us in many directions in our lives (and not just in our love lives!), whether or not we realize that it is sexual energy that moves us. Sexual energy is the pure and wild energy of creativity, with love the great balancer of impulse. When aligned with the calming influence of love, transmuted and then focused into other activities, sexual energy reveals itself as the key to achieving all goals.

For this reason, sexual energy is the most critical energy to get in touch and work with. When we are in sync with it we feel fully alive. The ebb and flow of the core of our sexuality enables us to really appreciate life and we experience ourselves differently. Once we are aware of it as our primary motivating force we can control and direct it to manifest our highest desires and goals, rather than being at its whim and urge. So don't be afraid of sexual energy. Work with it and use it! If you transmute your desire into another form (say, a project, sport or hobby) you are using your sexual energy to create. A true or 'burning' desire leads to creation on all levels, because the sex drive must first be engaged and channeled through the heart chakra (love) in order to bring forth creativity. How you use sexual energy is absolutely individual. But you will need time and practise to harness it properly before following through to achieve your desire.

Sensuality is appreciation and respect for life at every level. Sensuality is appreciation and respect for life at every level. Sensuality is appreciation and respect for life at every level. s

Sensuality is appreciation and respect for life at every level. Sensuality is appreciation and respect for life at every level. Sensuality is appreciation and respect for life. Sensuality is appreciation and respect for life

Sensuality

Sensuality is appreciation and respect for life at every level. Sensuality is more nurturing and sustaining than sexuality alone because it celebrates abundance in the realm of the senses, as well as love and respect, rather than sheer physicality. Sensuality is the extra 'x-factor' that brings the highest form of physical love. Don't confuse sexuality with sensuality – they often dance to different tunes. But they can dance together, if you are aware not just of your body but your spirit and the world around you. Then you are serving the highest purpose of God and the Universe. Sensuality develops as you grow, which is why it is wise to wait as long as possible before engaging in the physical expression of love. Through understanding sensuality you can understand that you are here, not merely to pick at the offerings on the table of life, but to gorge yourself, enjoying every morsel and not wasting any of its pleasures. It's your responsibility to do so. Women are the custodians of sensuality, providing much of what is sensual in the world. So respect sensuality: nurture it, direct it, lead others to it and enjoy its rewards.

kama sutra = love lessons

Of all the kinds of love, we are most tested by physical love. We might wonder whether we are simply residing in the lower chakras: is it a purely functional activity devoid of or lacking the necessary emotional and mental content? Or are we overintellectualizing: are we coming from the higher chakras and ignoring what's in our heart? The heart chakra is the great mediator, keeping our physical desires and our mental agendas in perfect balance. If we come from the heart then the physical form of love is appropriate in all its beauty. This is how the Universe intended for us to enter into physicality. The heart is the real gateway to intimacy.

Dressing is not just a matter of expressing yourself or a question of taste. It's also about effectiveness. So you don't need to reveal all when you go out. Day or night, the sexiest thing in the world is what can't be seen, or what is only discreetly and artfully revealed. While it's great for the beach, in other settings letting it all hang out can look desperate. That goes for anyone.

How you dress can also dictate how others relate to you. The energy that you put out is what you'll pull in. Maximize your chances of meeting a kindred spirit or at least one who relates to you on more than just a physical level. Don't go out with all of your wares on display – keep a few in reserve! Besides, reality can rarely compare to another person's imagination, which is probably the biggest turn on of all.

'Imagination is more important

| Albert Einstein

CLEAVAGE

than knowledge'

Sacred sex

Sex should never be a pressured situation – it's about trust ...and fun! There are no medals for performance and everyone's a winner. It's an intensely private and personal experience. Sex should be as beautiful as it is both energizing and relaxed. You're meant to enjoy it, not just endure it.

Love rules

When it comes to the so-called rules about intimate relationships with men, the only rule is that there are no rules. Men feel the same emotions, fears and insecurities as women do. In the love arena, which is the biggest arena of all, there are no winners or losers. No one is superior. Everyone needs courage to enter. Isolationists don't survive. Only the gladiators who stick together survive.

A kiss is never

just a kiss

There's a whole universe of meaning contained in a kiss.

CHEMISTRY

When you are with someone for a while you find that you have absorbed their essence or their vibe. They are having an effect on your body chemistry. This happens gradually, often without either of you being aware. It's as if you are both living together in a bubble. You can often see it in older couples who have been together for a long period of time. They share mannerisms and verbal expressions, even various physical attributes. It is likely that the changes we can see on the outside have also happened underneath. This is why when you spend a lot of time with someone, they are 'in' you more than you may be aware of. Their aura has fused with yours. So when you separate or break-up you miss them, at best, or at worst you feel anxiety or depression. What you're experiencing is a withdrawal as your body craves the reaction that is generated by the other

LESSONS
The alchemy of breaking up

person's presence. It's another reason why getting over a break-up and having no contact with a former partner hurts like hell. Going cold turkey is the fastest remedy. The best thing you can do is accept the situation as soon as possible. Don't unnecessarily prolong the closure process: it will only cause more pain and possibly permanent damage. And don't waste time or hinder your progress. Recognize that this was most probably a karmic relationship that has run its course. Forgive and forge ahead. If you can understand what it was that led you into the relationship and what you learned from it, you'll quickly gain a new perspective, not only of the other person but also (and more importantly) of yourself. And if there is a destiny that you are meant to share, in the future it will manifest, if and when the time is right.

surrender to

surrender to your bliss surrender to your bliss surrender to your bliss surrender to your bliss surrender to g

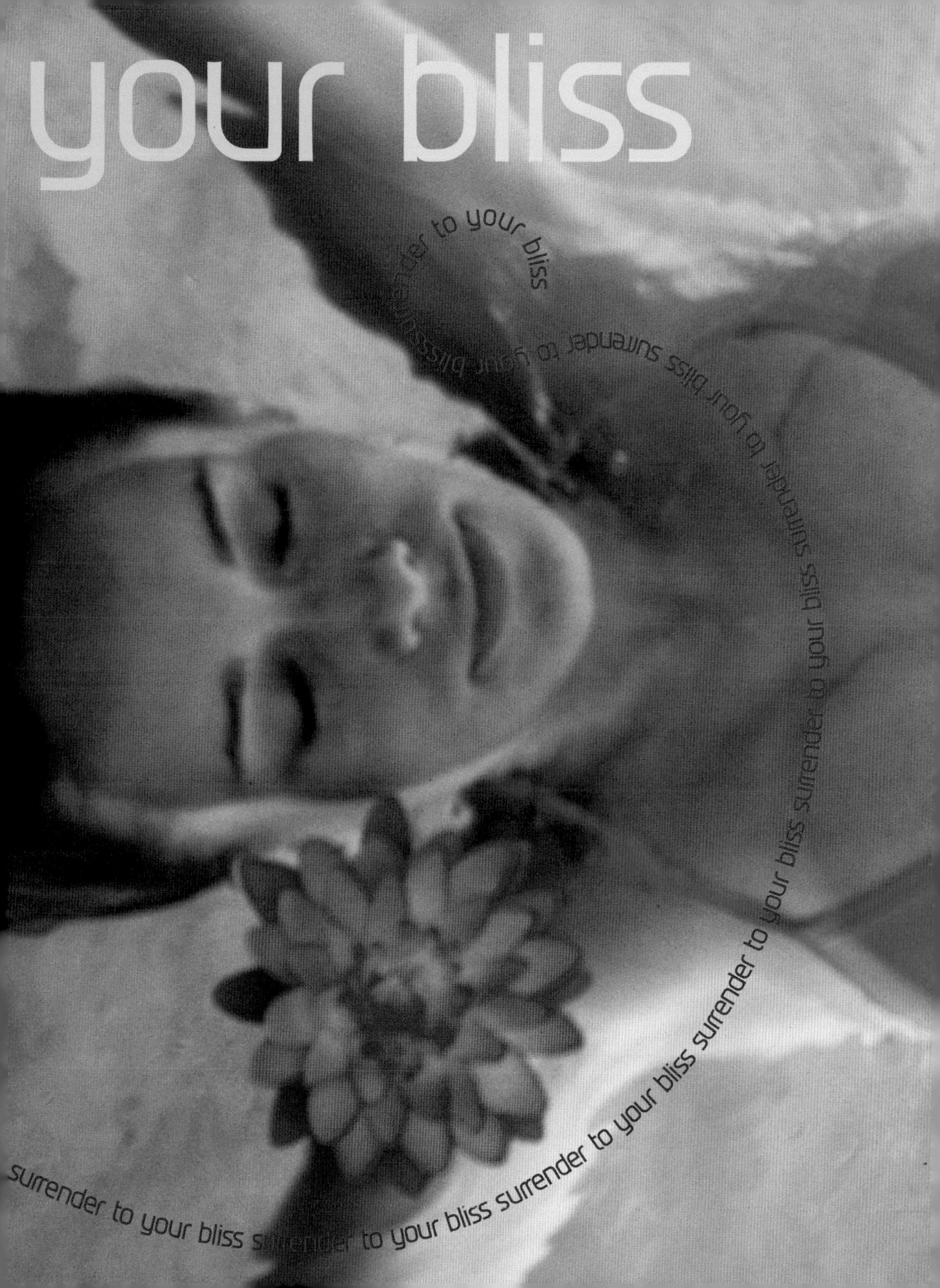

your bliss
surrender to your bliss surrender to your bliss surrender to your bliss surrender to your bliss surrender to your bliss surrender to your bliss surrender to your bliss surrender to your bliss

INTENSITY
LEADS TO
VULNERABILITY
LEADS TO
STRENGTH

kiss my

feet

desire

destiny
enters
source
impulses
rule
everything

CHAKRA: **solar plexus chakra**: integration of personality, alignment of impulses, free will, wishes and personal power

[def:n] To wish or long for; to crave; to want; to possess; to express a wish to obtain; to ask for; from a person or from the Universe; the force that binds the individual to the cycle of karma; to send thought energy regarding an activity or situation that you would like to happen.

If you really want to experience love, you have to take a risk.

Love's always worth the risk.

Wishing well

A child's wish is intense, and the Universe never ignores such powerful thought energy. Your childhood dreams will invariably lead to your true path in life if you stay true to yourself and your heart. Even if the path seems random and without reason or far from the original dream, your dreams will manifest.

T LOVE FUTURE LOVE STAR LOVE SILENT LOVE GLOBAL LOVE YOUR LOVE WILD LOVE MESSAGE OF LOVE BABY LO
E MY LOVE LOVE RULES MONEY LOVE PAST LOVE VIRTUAL LOVE TAINTED LOVE SACRED LOVE LOVE SAGA LOVE
E PARENTAL LOVE LOVE PLAY UNREQUITED LOVE SELF LOVE INDEPENDENT LOVE PUPPY LOVE ROAD TO LOVE H
E TALK CONDITIONAL LOVE BODY OF LOVE LOVE CYCLE LOOK OF LOVE PATERNAL LOVE ANIMAL LOVE LOVE AGAI
RITUAL LOVE FAMILY LOVE KARMIC LOVE LOVE CHILD PREDESTINED LOVE LOVE SUCKS UNCONDITIONAL LOVE SU
E HIGH FAST LOVE FUTURE LOVE STAR LOVE SILENT LOVE GLOBAL LOVE YOUR LOVE WILD LOVE MESSAGE OF LO
E SWEET LOVE MY LOVE LOVE RULES MONEY LOVE PAST LOVE VIRTUAL LOVE TAINTED LOVE SACRED LOVE LOVE
RBIDDEN LOVE PARENTAL LOVE LOVE PLAY UNREQUITED LOVE SELF LOVE INDEPENDENT LOVE PUPPY LOVE ROAD
AL LOVE LOVE TALK CONDITIONAL LOVE BODY OF LOVE LOVE CYCLE LOOK OF LOVE PATERNAL LOVE ANIMAL LOVE
D LOVE SPIRITUAL LOVE FAMILY LOVE KARMIC LOVE LOVE CHILD PREDESTINED LOVE LOVE SUCKS UNCONDITIONA
NOT LOVE HIGH FAST LOVE FUTURE LOVE STAR LOVE SILENT LOVE GLOBAL LOVE YOUR LOVE WILD LOVE MESS
TONIC LOVE SWEET LOVE MY LOVE LOVE RULES MONEY LOVE PAST LOVE VIRTUAL LOVE TAINTED LOVE SACRED
INE LOVE FORBIDDEN LOVE PARENTAL LOVE LOVE PLAY UNREQUITED LOVE SELF LOVE INDEPENDENT LOVE PUP
NDENT LOVE IDEAL LOVE LOVE TALK CONDITIONAL LOVE BODY OF LOVE LOVE CYCLE LOOK OF LOVE PATERNAL L
E HIGHER LOVE OLD LOVE SPIRITUAL LOVE FAMILY LOVE KARMIC LOVE LOVE CHILD PREDESTINED LOVE LOVE S
E LOVE STYLE LOVE ME NOT LOVE HIGH FAST LOVE FUTURE LOVE STAR LOVE SILENT LOVE GLOBAL LOVE YOUR L
E ME ONE LOVE PLATONIC LOVE SWEET LOVE MY LOVE LOVE RULES MONEY LOVE PAST LOVE VIRTUAL LOVE TAIN
ME REAL LOVE DIVINE LOVE FORBIDDEN LOVE PARENTAL LOVE LOVE PLAY UNREQUITED LOVE SELF LOVE INDEPEN
RTS CODEPENDENT LOVE IDEAL LOVE LOVE TALK CONDITIONAL LOVE BODY OF LOVE LOVE CYCLE LOOK OF LOVE
G IDOL LOVE HIGHER LOVE OLD LOVE SPIRITUAL LOVE FAMILY LOVE KARMIC LOVE LOVE CHILD PREDESTINED LO
NITE LOVE LOVE STYLE LOVE ME NOT LOVE HIGH FAST LOVE FUTURE LOVE STAR LOVE SILENT LOVE GLOBAL LO
ICE LOVE LOVE ME ONE LOVE PLATONIC LOVE SWEET LOVE MY LOVE LOVE RULES MONEY LOVE PAST LOVE VIRTL
ACK LOVE GAME REAL LOVE DIVINE LOVE FORBIDDEN LOVE PARENTAL LOVE LOVE PLAY UNREQUITED LOVE SELF
BOO LOVE HURTS CODEPENDENT LOVE IDEAL LOVE LOVE TALK CONDITIONAL LOVE BODY OF LOVE LOVE CYCLE L
ART LOVE BUG IDOL LOVE HIGHER LOVE OLD LOVE SPIRITUAL LOVE FAMILY LOVE KARMIC LOVE LOVE CHILD PRED
RVIVAL INFINITE LOVE LOVE STYLE LOVE ME NOT LOVE HIGH FAST LOVE FUTURE LOVE STAR LOVE SILENT LOVE
NG-DISTANCE LOVE LOVE ME ONE LOVE PLATONIC LOVE SWEET LOVE MY LOVE LOVE RULES MONEY LOVE PAST
E LOVE SHACK LOVE GAME REAL LOVE DIVINE LOVE FORBIDDEN LOVE PARENTAL LOVE LOVE PLAY UNREQUITED
WER LOVE TABOO LOVE HURTS CODEPENDENT LOVE IDEAL LOVE LOVE TALK CONDITIONAL LOVE BODY OF LOVE
E SICK LOVE HEART LOVE BUG IDOL LOVE HIGHER LOVE OLD LOVE SPIRITUAL LOVE FAMILY LOVE KARMIC LOVE
LIDAY LOVE LOVE SURVIVAL INFINITE LOVE LOVE STYLE LOVE ME NOT LOVE HIGH FAST LOVE FUTURE LOVE STAR
ASE LOVE SEAT LONG-DISTANCE LOVE LOVE ME ONE LOVE PLATONIC LOVE SWEET LOVE MY LOVE LOVE RULES
N LOVE MOTHER LOVE LOVE SHACK LOVE GAME REAL LOVE DIVINE LOVE FORBIDDEN LOVE PARENTAL LOVE LOV
CRET LOVE LOVE POWER LOVE TABOO LOVE HURTS CODEPENDENT LOVE IDEAL LOVE LOVE TALK CONDITIONAL L
E LOVE HATE LOVE SICK LOVE HEART LOVE BUG IDOL LOVE HIGHER LOVE OLD LOVE SPIRITUAL LOVE FAMILY L
E TRUE LOVE HOLIDAY LOVE LOVE SURVIVAL INFINITE LOVE LOVE STYLE LOVE ME NOT LOVE HIGH LOVE AGAIN LO
AL LOVE FAMILY LOVE KARMIC LOVE LOVE CHILD PREDESTINED LOVE LOVE SUCKS UNCONDITIONAL LOVE SUMM
GH FAST LOVE FUTURE LOVE STAR LOVE SILENT LOVE GLOBAL LOVE YOUR LOVE WILD LOV E MESSAGE OF LOVE
EET LOVE MY LOVE LOVE RULES MONEY LOVE PAST LOVE VIRTUAL LOVE TAINTED LOVE SACRED LOVE LOVE SAG
DEN LOVE PARENTAL LOVE LOVE PLAY UNREQUITED LOVE SELF LOVE INDEPENDENT LOVE PUPPY LOVE ROAD TO

J OF LOVE FOOL FOR LOVE LOVE PHASE LOVE SEAT LONG DISTANCE LOVE LOVE ME ONE LOVE PLATONIC LOVE SW
UL LOVE WORLDLY LOVE HIDDEN LOVE MOTHER LOVE LOVE SHACK LOVE GAME REAL LOVE DIVINE LOVE FORBIDDE
LOVE THING PERFECT LOVE SECRET LOVE LOVE POWER LOVE TABOO LOVE HURTS CODEPENDENT LOVE IDEAL LO
TORY NEW LOVE MATERNAL LOVE LOVE HATE LOVE SICK LOVE HEART LOVE BUG IDOL LOVE HIGHER LOVE OLD LO
OVE FIRST LOVE ENDLESS LOVE TRUE LOVE HOLIDAY LOVE LOVE SURVIVAL INFINITE LOVE LOVE STYLE LOVE ME N
LOVE VISION OF LOVE FOOL FOR LOVE LOVE PHASE LOVE SEAT LONG-DISTANCE LOVE LOVE ME ONE LOVE PLATO
VE CHAIN SOUL LOVE WORLDLY LOVE HIDDEN LOVE MOTHER LOVE LOVE SHACK LOVE GAME REAL LOVE DIVINE LO
E HOT LOVE LOVE THING PERFECT LOVE SECRET LOVE LOVE POWER LOVE TABOO LOVE HURTS CODEPENDENT LO
AIN LOVE STORY NEW LOVE MATERNAL LOVE LOVE HATE LOVE SICK LOVE HEART LOVE BUG IDOL LOVE HIGHER LO
UMMER LOVE FIRST LOVE ENDLESS LOVE TRUE LOVE HOLIDAY LOVE LOVE SURVIVAL INFINITE LOVE LOVE STYLE LO
OVE BABY LOVE VISION OF LOVE FOOL FOR LOVE LOVE PHASE LOVE SEAT LONG-DISTANCE LOVE LOVE ME ONE LO
VE SAGA LOVE CHAIN SOUL LOVE WORLDLY LOVE HIDDEN LOVE MOTHER LOVE LOVE SHACK LOVE GAME REAL LO
ROAD TO LOVE HOT LOVE LOVE THING PERFECT LOVE SECRET LOVE LOVE POWER LOVE TABOO LOVE HURTS CC
IAL LOVE LOVE AGAIN LOVE STORY NEW LOVE MATERNAL LOVE LOVE HATE LOVE SICK LOVE HEART LOVE BUG I
NCONDITIONAL LOVE SUMMER LOVE FIRST LOVE ENDLESS LOVE TRUE LOVE HOLIDAY LOVE LOVE SURVIVAL INFIN
LOVE MESSAGE OF LOVE BABY LOVE VISION OF LOVE FOOL FOR LOVE LOVE PHASE LOVE SEAT LONG-DISTANCE L
E SACRED LOVE LOVE SAGA LOVE CHAIN SOUL LOVE WORLDLY LOVE HIDDEN LOVE MOTHER LOVE LOVE SHACK L
VE PUPPY LOVE ROAD TO LOVE HOT LOVE LOVE THING PERFECT LOVE SECRET LOVE LOVE POWER LOVE TABOO L
L LOVE ANIMAL LOVE LOVE AGAIN LOVE STORY NEW LOVE MATERNAL LOVE LOVE HATE LOVE SICK LOVE HEART L
SUCKS UNCONDITIONAL LOVE SUMMER LOVE FIRST LOVE ENDLESS LOVE TRUE LOVE HOLIDAY LOVE LOVE SURVI
OVE WILD LOVE MESSAGE OF LOVE BABY LOVE VISION OF LOVE FOOL FOR LOVE LOVE PHASE LOVE SEAT LONG-
TAINTED LOVE SACRED LOVE LOVE SAGA LOVE CHAIN SOUL LOVE WORLDLY LOVE HIDDEN LOVE MOTHER LOVE L
PENDENT LOVE PUPPY LOVE ROAD TO LOVE HOT LOVE LOVE THING PERFECT LOVE SECRET LOVE LOVE POWER L
VE PATERNAL LOVE ANIMAL LOVE LOVE AGAIN LOVE STORY NEW LOVE MATERNAL LOVE LOVE HATE LOVE SICK L
LOVE LOVE SUCKS UNCONDITIONAL LOVE SUMMER LOVE FIRST LOVE ENDLESS LOVE TRUE LOVE HOLIDAY LOVE L
VE YOUR LOVE WILD LOVE MESSAGE OF LOVE BABY LOVE VISION OF LOVE FOOL FOR LOVE LOVE PHASE LOVE S
UAL LOVE TAINTED LOVE SACRED LOVE LOVE SAGA LOVE CHAIN SOUL LOVE WORLDLY LOVE HIDDEN LOVE MOTH
F LOVE INDEPENDENT LOVE PUPPY LOVE ROAD TO LOVE HOT LOVE LOVE THING PERFECT LOVE SECRET LOVE L
CLE LOOK OF LOVE PATERNAL LOVE ANIMAL LOVE LOVE AGAIN LOVE STORY NEW LOVE MATERNAL LOVE LOVE H
LD PREDESTINED LOVE LOVE SUCKS UNCONDITIONAL LOVE SUMMER LOVE FIRST LOVE ENDLESS LOVE TRUE L
NT LOVE GLOBAL LOVE YOUR LOVE WILD LOVE MESSAGE OF LOVE BABY LOVE VISION OF LOVE FOOL FOR LOVE L
VE PAST LOVE VIRTUAL LOVE TAINTED LOVE SACRED LOVE LOVE SAGA LOVE CHAIN SOUL LOVE WORLDLY LOVE
REQUITED LOVE SELF LOVE INDEPENDENT LOVE PUPPY LOVE ROAD TO LOVE HOT LOVE LOVE THING PERFECT L
OF LOVE LOVE CYCLE LOOK OF LOVE PATERNAL LOVE ANIMAL LOVE LOVE AGAIN LOVE STORY NEW LOVE MATER
C LOVE LOVE CHILD PREDESTINED LOVE LOVE SUCKS UNCONDITIONAL LOVE SUMMER LOVE FIRST LOVE ENDL
NEW LOVE MATERNAL LOVE LOVE HATE LOVE SICK LOVE HEART LOVE BUG IDOL LOVE HIGHER LOVE OLD LOVE S
IRST LOVE ENDLESS LOVE TRUE LOVE HOLIDAY LOVE LOVE SURVIVAL INFINITE LOVE LOVE STYLE LOVE ME NOT L
VISION OF LOVE FOOL FOR LOVE LOVE PHASE LOVE SEAT LONG-DISTANCE LOVE LOVE ME ONE LOVE PLATONIC L
AIN SOUL LOVE WORLDLY LOVE HIDDEN LOVE MOTHER LOVE LOVE SHACK LOVE GAME REAL LOVE DIVINE LOVE F
LOVE LOVE THING PERFECT LOVE SECRET LOVE LOVE POWER FAST LOVE FUTURE LOVE STAR LOVE SILENT LOV

Picture perfect

The question is not is he or she
perfect? That's not the issue.
The real question is: are you
perfect for each other? And
don't compare anyone new with
your previous partners either.
They are all in your past and
there's a reason for that.
Focus on the present and the
potential in that for your future.
Who's in the picture RIGHT
HERE, RIGHT NOW.

Desire versus love

How do you tell the difference between desire and love? Emotions run high in both instances, so what's the decisive factor?

Desire that is pure lust seeks only one outcome – physical gratification. Once it becomes apparent to someone who is in lust, not love, that their desire may not be gratified, they usually lose interest or begin to pursue their next target. But love sticks around for the secret ingredient, the next level of spiritual uplift, above and beyond the instant hit of lust.

That's not to say that one can only exist without the other: love that incorporates desire is the ultimate in an intimate relationship.

But the desire factor can confuse you both. So to clear the channels and see if it's love or desire you're both feeling, take your time. Wait and see. Be on the lookout for the giveaway signals. Do they still want to hang around? Do you? Do they like you as a person? Do they show interest in you as an individual rather than as the sum total of your body parts? Time is the test of love and the revealer of the true nature of desire.

Sometimes what seems

real is really fake.

Addicted to...?

Addicts are lost souls. They are people for whom something went seriously wrong. There may appear to be many reasons why an individual becomes an addict or involved in any form of substance abuse. But we can never fully comprehend what's gone wrong. We can only try to mend, and it may or may not be possible. Typically an addict has either crumbled under the weight of expectations (theirs or someone else's) or has lost faith in their ability to be able to live their dreams or in the Universe's ability to take the burden for them - they lose faith. They need our love and compassion, not our derision, scorn or punishment, for they have punished themselves enough. They are living out a destiny of pain and despair caused by their own lost self-love and their disconnection from the abundance of love that is all around them.

Affairs of the heart

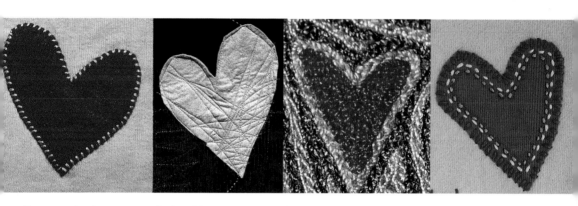

If you embark upon a relationship or have an affair with someone who is already involved, be warned: life will ensure that at some point you too will be on the receiving end of deception in a love affair. Even if you rationalize your affair as 'just a fling', there will be consequences. Like karma, for instance. You will always have a nagging feeling that it may happen again – to you, this time. After all, how can you expect your partner to be faithful to you if your relationship began with unfaithfulness? Your life may become, in the words of the poet Philip Larkin, 'a life that cannot climb clear of its wrong beginnings', and you will have led each other to believe that infidelity is acceptable behavior. Affairs are dishonest and devastating for all concerned and they can ruin lives. They are all about avoidance, which is based on fear: fear of being honest, fear of confronting truth, fear of ultimate surrender and commitment. Having an affair is a cowardly way to take control or to win back a sense of power that perhaps was lost along the way. In any case, an affair rarely results in a satisfying, long-term commitment, because affairs are all about avoiding commitment. Even if your affair does work out, the relationship began with deception. This may have major consequences for the trust that each of you will need if your relationship is to truly succeed. Because trust holds relationships together. Love alone can't do it. Without trust and love an affair of the heart will always be an affair without heart.

The best trainers in the world won't help you if you don't have a winning attitude.

" In order to win you must expect to win "

Diamonds are **not** a girl's best friend

You don't need someone to give you a diamond ring in order to feel worthy or lovable. If you really think that wearing a ring on your fourth finger somehow makes you a better person, don't wait for someone else to give you one. Don't waste any more time: give one to yourself — immediately!

be your own best friend

food (f)or love

The love of food is one of the great physical joys in life, a sensory byproduct of an essential activity. Food has always been associated with love, and the feeding of loved ones, whether by a parent to a child or lover to a partner, is one of the ways we show our love to each other as humans.

It's also one way we show love to ourselves – and one way we withhold it. Our bodies need regular amounts of good, wholesome food and giving nourishment to them is an important way to love ourselves.

But if we become too focused on food and eating we may develop an obsession, and obsessions are rarely healthy. When we are in emotional and physical balance we know what feels good to eat and how much food is enough. But when our emotional needs send mixed signals to our physical body food addictions, cravings or hunger denial can spiral out of control.

It's all about what food represents to each of us personally. So what does food mean to you? Food is something to be experienced as a part of life. But for some people it's only when they remember it. It's simply not a high priority on their list. Do you relate to that mindset or is eating an event that consumes all of your waking moments? Is food your enemy, the one thing that you fear, a permanent test of your willpower and a reminder of your 'weakness'? And do you believe you are a better person if you 'go without', and that this somehow reflects your self-discipline and control over your body? In the West there is no lack of food, so what is lacking? Are you craving love and using food to fill yourself up? Do you think you are worthy of love?

Be honest with yourself. Use your 'food craving index' as a gauge of where you are emotionally. How much love do you have for yourself and for others? Do you actually believe that you are lovable? When you feel the urge to eat too much or too little, try to shift the focus from your stomach to your mind: what's really going on for you? Are you under pressure and feeling unloved or just feeling lonely? Are you angry – at yourself, your parents, your partners? Who are you trying to punish? And who really gets punished when you don't respect your body's needs? What do you really want in life? Can you see the link between your attitude towards food or eating and your personal view of yourself? These are all tough questions, but you can learn a lot about yourself by attempting to answer them honestly.

Replace obsessive thoughts of food with ideas. Express desire, don't ingest it: use your desire for food to channel your real desires. For wherever there is desire there is also creativity. And wherever there is creativity there is love. And plenty of it, too.

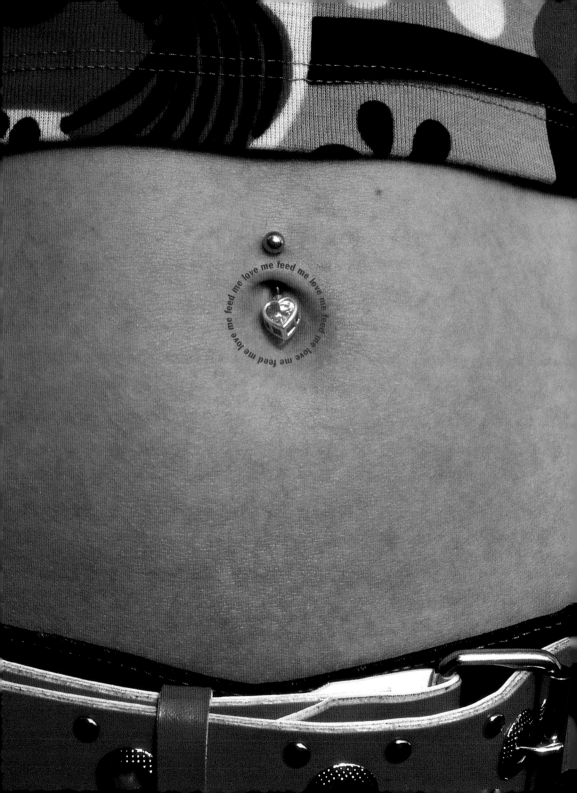

Forget the formula

NEVER THINK THAT YOUR LIFE CAN BE FORMULARIZED: THAT YOU CAN ALWAYS HAVE THE PERFECT HOUSE, JOB, FAMILY, RELATIONSHIPS, WARDROBE. YOU MAY EXPERIENCE WHAT SEEM TO BE MOMENTS OF PERFECTION, BUT THE AIRBRUSHED LIFESTYLE IS A MYTH.

THE REALITY OF LIFE, WITH ITS CHAOS AND DISAPPOINTMENTS, JOYS AND UNEXPECTED TWISTS AND CHANGES, IS MUCH MORE INTERESTING. IT DOESN'T MATTER WHAT EVERYONE ELSE THINKS OF YOUR LIFE, LIFESTYLE, CAREER, BOYFRIEND, FRIENDS OR FAMILY – IT'S WHAT YOU THINK THAT'S IMPORTANT. IF YOU ENVY SOMEONE ELSE YOU WILL ALWAYS FEEL SECOND BEST.

LOVE YOUR LIFE. BECAUSE LOVE IS THE STATE OF MIND IN WHICH YOU CAN ACCEPT AND BE GRATEFUL FOR WHAT YOU HAVE.

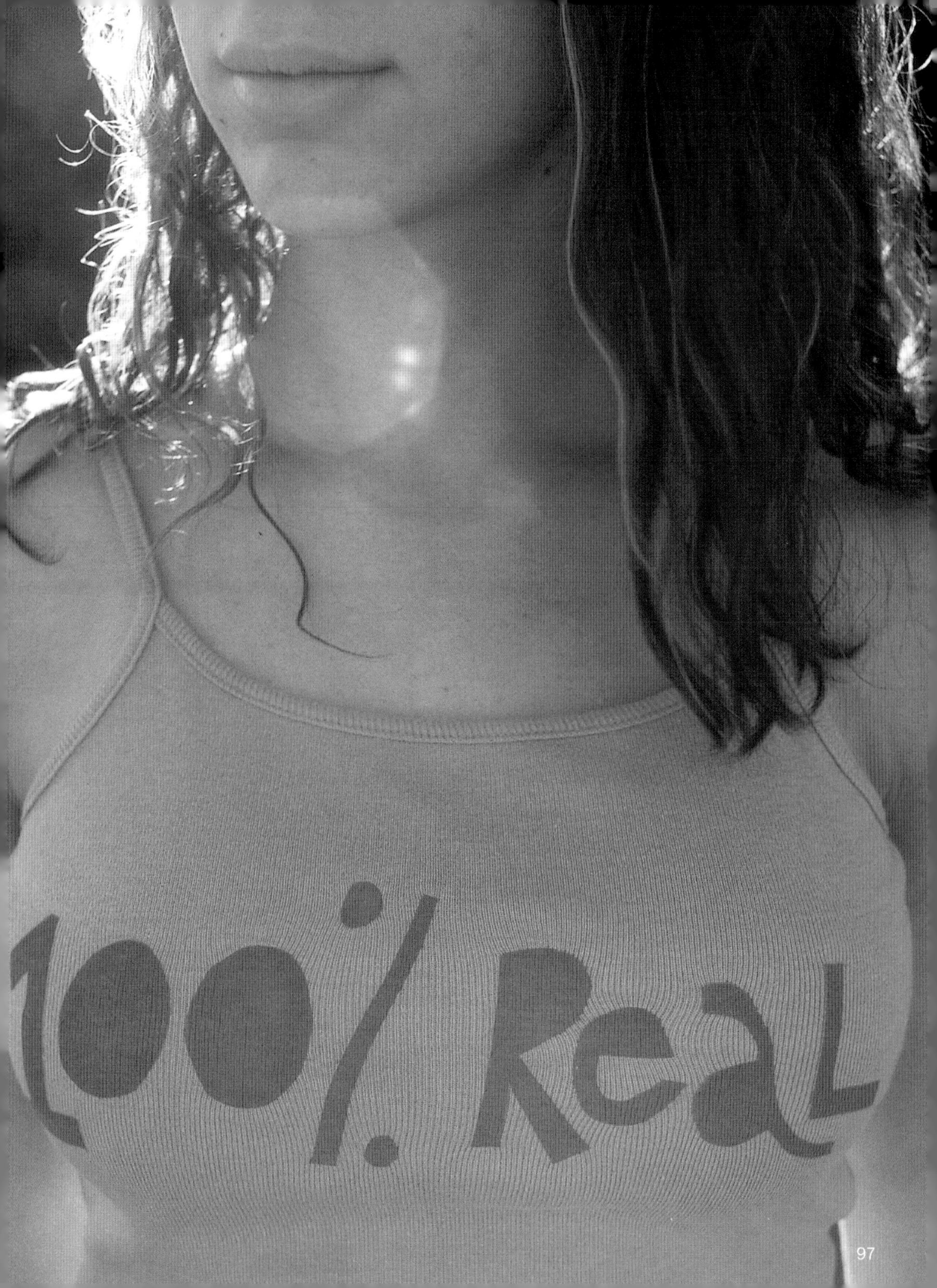
100% Real

OF LOVE = THE CROSS

THE ULTIMATE SYMBOL

THE CROSS = THE CROSSROADS OF YOUR LIFE

IT'S YOUR CHOICE

THE CROSS REPRESENTS THE PATH OF LOVE

EACH TIME IS A CHANCE TO GO THE WAY OF LOVE

Relation-ships

BEFORE YOU JUMP INTO A RELATIONSHIP WITH BOTH FEET, WAIT UNTIL THE OTHER PERSON IS WELL AND TRULY OVER THEIR PAST RELATIONSHIP IF THEY ARE STILL IN THE WASH-UP MODE OF DISENTANGLEMENT, IT'S BETTER TO HANG BACK. IT CAN BE TURBULENT IN THE WAKE OF ANOTHER SHIP'S DEPARTURE. BEST TO WAIT UNTIL THE WATERS ARE CALM ONCE AGAIN.

Halong Bay, Vietnam

IS YOUR LOVE LIFE

BEATING YOU UP?

Abuse is the symptom of a far deeper problem

If you are torturing someone or someone else is torturing you with verbal, psychological or physical abuse, it's time to put everything on hold. If you are the perpetrator of the abuse, you are obviously tortured and probably inflict similar abuse on yourself. Your own self-loathing is manifested inwardly and outwardly, and you must seek help to heal yourself.

If you're the one being abused, get out of victim mode – take massive action. Tell your family, neighbors, counseling service officers, police – anyone who can support you in whatever action you need to take. You can turn your life around at any time. No one owns you. Be strong and responsible for yourself and anyone in your care.

ABUSE OF ANY FORM IS COMPLETELY UNACCEPTABLE AT ANY TIME. IT'S SIMPLY NOT ON.

Abuse includes any form of harassment or intimidation, verbal or physical, and any tactics like threats or blackmail. If it feels threatening, it is, and there are **NO EXCUSES** for this behavior. If you find yourself in a situation you can't control or where you are afraid: GET OUT IMMEDIATELY. You need care and support — and they need help too.

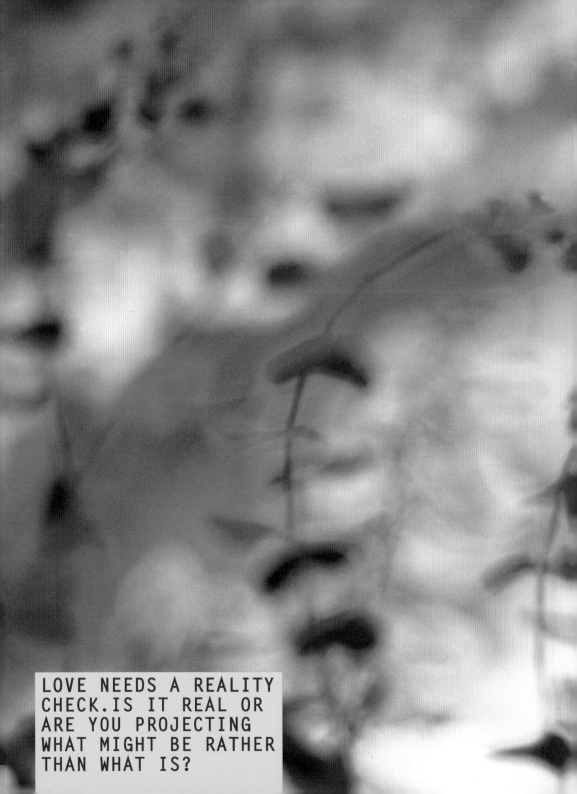

LOVE NEEDS A REALITY
CHECK.IS IT REAL OR
ARE YOU PROJECTING
WHAT MIGHT BE RATHER
THAN WHAT IS?

WILD ANIMALS CAN HURT YOU WHEN THEY ARE AFRAID YOU'RE GOING TO HURT THEM FIRST. BUT IF YOU APPROACH THEM GENTLY, WITHOUT FEAR OR EXCITEMENT, THEY ARE UNLIKELY TO. PEOPLE ARE THE SAME. GO GENTLY.

dream on

'. . . go in pursuit of your dream. The dunes are changed by the wind, but the desert never changes. That's the way it will be with our love for each other. Maktub [It is written] if I am really a part of your dream, you'll come back one day.'

Paulo Coelho, *The Alchemist*

Remember:
nothing goes
by you that's
for you.

heart

healing

emotions

affirm

real

truth

CHAKRA: **heart chakra**: of feeling, healing and emotions; free will and intuition are balanced by free-flowing love; the processor and mediator between the higher and lower energies of the chakras above and below to create recognition of the eternal in all that is physical

[def:n] A hollow muscular organ which keeps the blood in circulation throughout the body; the seat of life and of vital powers of thought, feeling and emotion; the essential part or core; the center of the emotions and affections (in contrast to the head as the seat of intellect); sensibility; capacity or sympathy; the root of compassion.

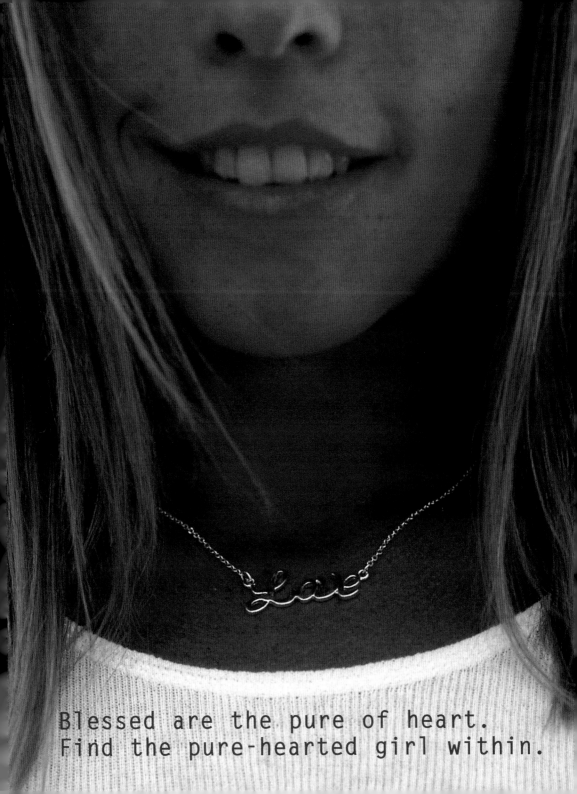

Blessed are the pure of heart.
Find the pure-hearted girl within.

LOVE IS PERMANENT.
IT STAYS IN THE HEART.
ONCE YOU HAVE HAD IT, YOU
CAN HAVE IT AGAIN.

114

An act of love

is one that comes directly from the heart for no reason other than to fulfil itself, an action done just for the sake of it. Make each day count — one per day even in the smallest way.

A PHONE CALL A CARD A SINGLE KISS A SMILE FOR A STRANGER AN UNEXPECTED GIFT A CARING SHOULDER AN ARTICLE OF INTEREST A GENTLE REMINDER AN E-MAIL XOXO A TEXT MESSAGE A HELPING HAND A CURIOSITY DEVELOPED A FLOWER FOR A FRIEND A PRAYER A POSITIVE THOUGHT A CANDLE LIT A SURPRISE VISIT AN INTEREST SHOWN A MOMENT'S PEACE A FRIEND IN NEED A CONVERSATION FOLLOWED UP A COMPLIMENT PASSED ON AN ATTENTIVE EAR A JOB UNSEEN A REFERRAL AN I LOVE YOU

To be
a princess

is to play at life. To be a queen is to be a serious player...Most of us are a little of both. The purpose of life as a woman is to ascend to the throne and rule with heart.'

Marianne Williamson, *A Woman's Worth*

LIKE ANYTHING, THE THEORY OF LOVE CAN BE LEARNED. YOU CAN LEARN TO RECOGNIZE IT, EVEN UNDERSTAND IT, BY READING DESCRIPTIONS IN BOOKS, WATCHING FILMS OR HEARING THE LOVE STORIES OF OTHER PEOPLE. BUT YOU CANNOT LEARN LOVE ONLY BY STUDYING THE THEORY. LIKE DRIVING, YOU HAVE TO DO IT — KNOW IT, FEEL IT AND ULTIMATELY EXPERIENCE IT. AND THEN YOU CAN TRULY GIVE IT. SO LIFT YOUR HEAD AND SEE THE BEAUTY AND LOVE IN THE WORLD AROUND YOU. THEN DO IT! LOVE IS NOT HARD TO FIND. LOVE IS HARD TO GIVE. YOU CANNOT DICTATE THE TERMS ON WHICH LOVE IS GIVEN. YOU CAN ONLY BE GRATEFUL FOR IT.

heart
of grass

love is in your own backyard

You are lovable

AS WE THINK, SO WE CREATE. OUR THOUGHTS CREATE OUR ENVIRONMENT. THIS INCLUDES OUR RELATIONSHIPS – WITH FAMILY, FRIENDS AND LOVERS. ALL THE PRECONCEPTIONS AND BELIEFS THAT WE MAY HAVE ABOUT OURSELVES AND OUR RELATIONSHIPS ADD UP TO WHEREVER WE FIND OURSELVES NOW. OUR PRESENT LIVES ARE REFLECTIONS OF ALL OUR PAST THOUGHT PROCESSES.

SO BE RESPONSIBLE WITH AND FOR YOUR THOUGHTS. WILL YOURSELF TO BELIEVE YOU ARE LOVED AND LOVABLE. PRACTICE ERASING ANY NEGATIVE BELIEFS YOU HAVE GATHERED: FIRST IDENTIFY THEM, THEN REPLACE THEM WITH POSITIVE AFFIRMATIONS.

AS LOUISE L. HAY SAYS, 'THE POINT OF POWER IS IN THE PRESENT MOMENT.' IN TIME AND WITH AWARENESS YOU WILL BEGIN TO OVERCOME THE PATTERNS THAT HAVE PREVENTED YOU FROM ACHIEVING THE SORTS OF RELATIONSHIPS THAT YOU TRULY DESIRE AND DESERVE.

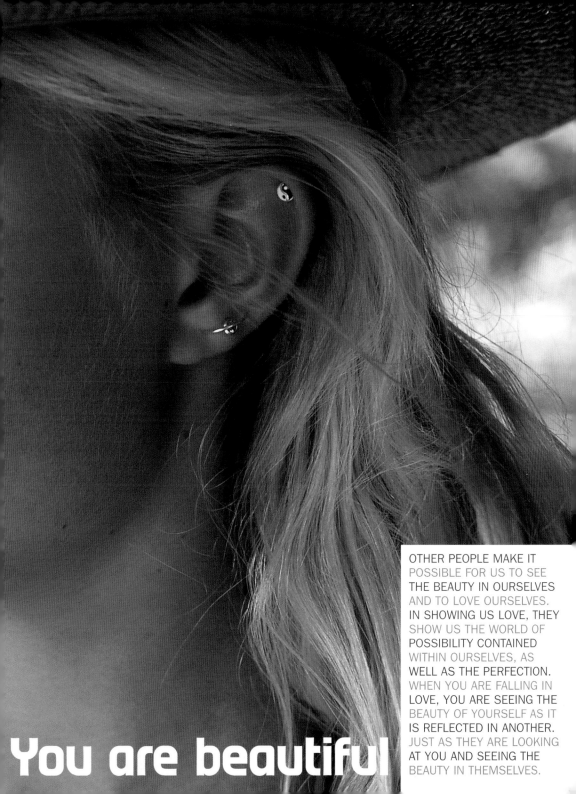

You are beautiful

OTHER PEOPLE MAKE IT POSSIBLE FOR US TO SEE THE BEAUTY IN OURSELVES AND TO LOVE OURSELVES. IN SHOWING US LOVE, THEY SHOW US THE WORLD OF POSSIBILITY CONTAINED WITHIN OURSELVES, AS WELL AS THE PERFECTION. WHEN YOU ARE FALLING IN LOVE, YOU ARE SEEING THE BEAUTY OF YOURSELF AS IT IS REFLECTED IN ANOTHER. JUST AS THEY ARE LOOKING AT YOU AND SEEING THE BEAUTY IN THEMSELVES.

Private lives

Keep your love life between you and your
partner. The world you have created is a sacred
space, a bubble designed for two. Privacy is a
precious gift. Only rarely allow others into your
space. Idle gossip about your private affairs
and activities can be very damaging to your
relationship, because you are depleting the
energy in your world. And on a human level,
you invite others to make value judgments
about the state of your relationship.
Give your relationship the best chance possible.
Keep it inside the heart, where it belongs.

Love means having to say sorry – a lot. It's also having to hear someone else's apology in turn. And then graciously accepting it.

125

love, no strings

When there are conditions attached to love – 'I love you if you'll . . .' or 'If you loved me you'd . . .' – it is no longer love. You cannot force someone to do certain things for you or to act in a particular way or to say the things you want them to, not even 'I love you'. Others do what they want most of the time, so if they don't call or they don't act in a caring way the best thing you can do is to simply observe it for what it is without any expectations. If you don't have expectations, then you can view most things as a bonus. This doesn't mean that you should put up with bad treatment but it does mean you can decide to love and accept each person as they present. And you can make choices as to what works best for you. Bringing it back to you and what you need means taking the focus off them – no blame, no victim. This is called loving unconditionally. Unconditional love is the ultimate test. The challenge is to see if we're really capable of loving without strings attached, the way we say we are. The question to ask is, 'Am I allowing fear to prevent me from loving without conditions and terms?' Because by transcending fear you can love unconditionally. In other words, you're in control, and you're not relying on someone else to feel loved or to be responsible for how you feel. You take responsibility for yourself and you allow others to be as they are. You can love some-one and still keep your power. This is unconditional love in action.

Family ties

We all know how important our close friends are to us. Often we may feel that we are best understood by our friends. Because friends are often the people most able to cut through to exactly where we are or what we're thinking.

Friendships are therefore critical indicators of how we see ourselves and how we see the world around us. Long-term friends can be as important to our sense of who we are as relatives, intimate partners or work colleagues.

Some friends are so close we consider them family, and this is one of the benefits of modern life. It's very common now for people to have their own definition of extended family, one which may include blood family and friends. An extended family provides a variety of inputs and consequently more opportunities for personal growth. When outsiders become insiders we are challenged differently and we get to know ourselves in a completely new context.

These relationships are deep and are very much based on love in action. They help us to become the best person we can.

Sisters: Catriona Dowding and Jess Gordon

Tolerance is total acceptance

Open your eyes.

of others' uniqueness.

Open your heart.

In the Game of Love, it's the way you play – not who wins – that counts. That's why it's a Love Game – when the score is nil all it's LOVE ALL.

Keep your heart open 24-7

Just because you think someone hurt or betrayed you doesn't mean you should shut down and harden your heart. Stay open and don't get bitter. Have faith in others and in yourself. It's just a test. What's your score? Often we think that by loving someone who has rejected us we have failed. But by loving without heed to the consequences you have passed the only test that counts. And besides, the Universe is keeping score. So don't worry any more. The point is not whether the love you gave was returned or not, it's that YOU LOVED. That is the most important thing.

love match vs

Havana — Cuba

grudge match

CONGRATULATIONS - you're a winner!

'In the depths of winter, within me there lay an

|Albert Camus

I finally learned that
invincible summer.

TO CREATE = TO GIVE
YOU CAN SHOW AND CREATE

POETRY WRITING LETTERS PHOTOGRAPHY

MOUNT DESCRIBE NOVEL STORY DEEP

AUDIO DOWNLOAD HANG FRAME POSTER

GROUP CANVAS COLLECTIVE RANGE

EXHIBITION BOOK MAGAZINE HANDPRINT

COLLECTION SCREENPLAY TREATMENT

PAINTING SCULPTURE FABRIC ARTISTIC

PERFORMANCE ART RALLY MUSIC REMIX

PAPER LINE DRAWINGS STUDIO IMAGE

TRANSPARENCY PHOTOPRINT PICTORIAL

BIRTH TO YOUR IDEAS
LOVE ANY TIME AT WILL:

DIRECTING CARDS ART COLLAGE LAYER

ETCH ESSAY PROGRAM ANIMATE FILM DUB

PRINT MULTIMEDIA MIX TAPE SESSIONS

SAMPLE SCREEN LIMITED EDITION PRINT

ILLUSTRATION WORD PLAY ACT SHOW

ONLINE THEME DOCUMENT ARTICLE

STATEMENT POLITICALLY ACTIVE

DIGITAL COMPRESSION WEB FILES

DETAIL PRESENTATION LOADING E-ZINE

RECORD LIST CONCEPT RE-CUT SPREAD

Love unexpressed is a crime against the heart.

Stranger in a

Each love relationship you enter is a doorway into a virtual reality that is unknown and untested. You step through this doorway armed with only one thing – faith. Faith is what makes love possible. For, having entered, you are each time a stranger in a strange land.

While love takes its course, faith will allow you to explore and be explored. At first the terrain will be unknown to you but gradually it will become more familiar. Anticipate the bends, look out for the valleys and head for the peaks, remembering that the unexpected can happen.

strange land

Lake Titicaca – Peru

The walls in your heart should be made of glass, so the light shines through.

emotion

every
moment
opens
to
intuition
over
negativity

CHAKRA: **throat chakra**: correlates to communication of emotions and regulates transition of the self towards inward reflections

[def.n] a state of consciousness in which joy, sadness, love, fear and other similar states of being are experienced; the effect on the senses of an event; a feeling which is the consequence of direct experience or the memory of an experience; the method of communication of the feelings associated with particular states of being.

je t'aime
ewedeshanno
aishite-imasu
te amo
ȯku ou ȯfa 'iate ƙoe
ewedeshanno
aloha
ȯku ou ȯfa 'iate ƙoe
phlâwt-ráƙ
amo-te
i love you
aloha
jag älskar dig
amo-te
je t'aime
saghapo
ich liebe dich
ewedeshanno
jag älskar dig
amo-te
ewedeshanno
phlâwt-ráƙ
ȯku ou ȯfa 'iate ƙoe
amo-te
i raakastan sinua
je t'aime
aishite-imasu
te amo
aloha
jag älskar dig
i love you
te amo
phlâwt-ráƙ
je t'aime
phlâwt-ráƙ
saghapo
te quiero
ȯku ou ȯfa 'iate ƙoe
ti amo
amo-te
te quiero
ich liebe dich
aloha
jag älskar dig
phlâwt-ráƙ
aishite-imasu
i love you
saghapo
aloha
saghapo
aloha
je t'aime
phlâwt-ráƙ
phlâwt-ráƙ
i love you
ti amo
aloha
je t'aime
amo-te
aloha
amo-te
je t'aime
ich liebe dich
phlâwt-ráƙ
ewedeshanno
i raakastan sinua
i love you
phlâwt-ráƙ
ȯku ou ȯfa 'iate ƙoe
amo-te
i love you
aloha
ai

i love you
phlâwt-ráƙ
aloha
amo-te
saghapo
te quiero
ich liebe dich
ewedeshanno
je t'aime
i love you
phlâwt-ráƙ
ti amo
i love you
i raakastan sinua
saghapo

The language of love is
the real language of the world.

in some ways we all need to hear the words 'I love you' but there are at least two schools of thought on this theory. One is the school which says to say it often, or as much as you can, or at least not to waste an opportunity to tell someone that you love them. The other school says to use these three words sparingly and that it renders them without meaning if you use them all the time. The truth probably lies somewhere in between; in any case it's all a question of degree. Telling someone you love them when you have only known them a short while may not be as intensely meaningful as telling a long-term partner or your parents. The point is that 'I love you' has as many meanings as there are moments – or individuals – and understood in this way we should all be free to express our individual version a lot more. There's no power in holding back and waiting for someone else to 'crack first'. Not telling someone that you love them could be one of the things you end up regretting in your life. Real power goes to whoever is able to communicate love. As it is often said, 'an ocean refuses no river'. The words 'I love you' are meant to be used – they're among the best ones we have. Don't wait too long.

Listen to the love around you. Your ears are open even if your mind is closed. How do you decode love? You must look, learn and listen. The signs of love are there.

make all communication

CLEAR

OPEN

HONEST

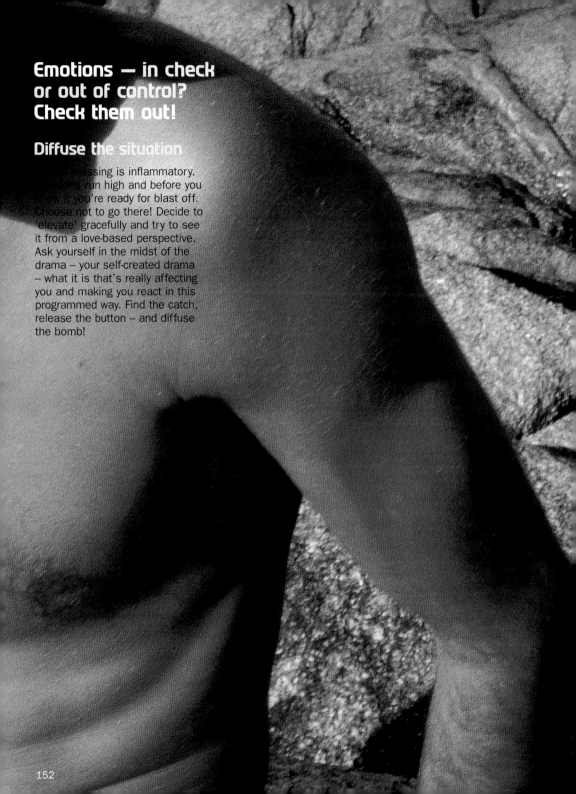

Emotions — in check or out of control? Check them out!

Diffuse the situation

...essing is inflammatory.
...s run high and before you
...w it you're ready for blast off.
Choose not to go there! Decide to
'elevate' gracefully and try to see
it from a love-based perspective.
Ask yourself in the midst of the
drama – your self-created drama
– what it is that's really affecting
you and making you react in this
programmed way. Find the catch,
release the button – and diffuse
the bomb!

love longing impatience irritation resentment no love

The (girlo) rules

If you must 'have it out' there are rules you need to follow:

1 Deal with it on neutral territory together (a park is a good place — the telephone isn't).

2 Stick to the issue at hand and the facts.

3 No name calling.

4 Keep it under control. Calm excessive emotion down.

5 Don't drag in past examples — it only shows you don't think you've got a strong case.

6 Elevate it — feel the real message. Where are the hurts? Who's hurting?

7 Put a time limit on the discussion and agree to reconvene if you go past it.

8 Forgive: yourself and them, irrespective of the outcome.

9 Ask: what would Love's response be?

The reasons

1 No manipulation ever worked or lasted for long.

2 No denial of gut feelings ever produced spiritual growth or real love.

3 No amount of game playing ever resulted in winners.

4 No amount of wanting ever achieved anything without a lesson attached.

5 No one can truly understand another person's reality.

6 No one can ever predict the outcome of anything with certainty.

7 No one will go by you who's meant for you.

If you mess up, 'fess up. Get back on track with honesty and a desire to do better. Forgiveness will come if you are sorry without qualification. Forgiveness is essential. We all need to forgive and to be forgiven. No excuses — sorry alone is all that's needed.

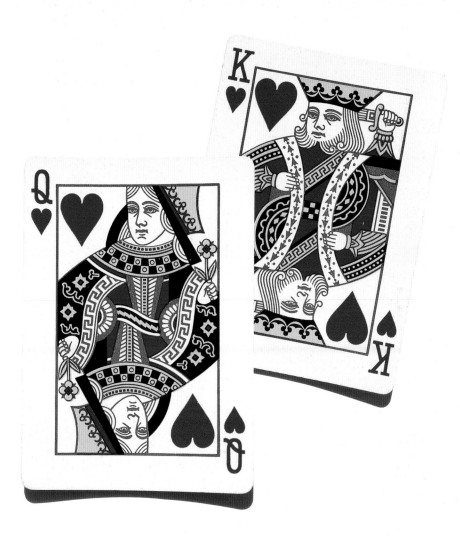

I am willing and able
So I throw
my cards on
your table.

| Bob Marley, 'Is This Love?'

THE BEST THING IS KNOWING

EXACTLY WHERE YOU STAND

Long-distance love

There are many reasons why we embark on or continue these seemingly illogical relationships. Perhaps one of you is transferred for work or goes away to study or travel. Maybe you met each other while you were traveling and you're seeing if there's anything in it.

Depending on the specifics of the situation a long-distance relationship can be a mixed blessing at best and downright challenging at worst. Deciding to conduct a relationship over a long distance is usually a gutsy call and not for those who lack courage or independence. There are sure to be difficulties, and the stress of being apart for important moments can test anyone.

The only way to manage a long-distance relationship is via communication, which is probably why you've become involved in this kind of relationship in the first place. Because a long-distance relationship will make you face up to your deepest fears: of abandonment, fidelity, learning to overcome or deal with jealousy and, of course, loneliness. There's only one solution: through clear, open and honest communication you both need to develop an understanding of what each expects and where you're (hopefully) going with it. The phone is a poor substitute, but when it's all you've got you'd both better learn to give good phone.

The effort to sustain a long-distance relationship is often too much for many people, but if you can step up to the plate and keep the channels of communication open, the excitement of reunions makes it worth it.

FACE OFF

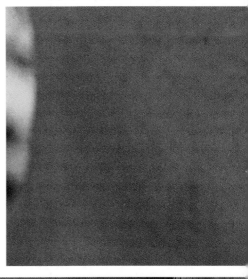

DON'T JUDGE A SITUATION UNTIL YOU ARE FACE TO FACE. MAKE NO ASSUMPTIONS ABOUT SOMEONE'S ACTIONS OR THOUGHTS UNTIL THEY ARE SITTING RIGHT THERE IN FRONT OF YOU TELLING YOU SOMETHING. REACH INSIDE YOURSELF AND FEEL WHETHER THEY ARE BEING HONEST WITH YOU. AND BE HONEST WITH YOURSELF: EVEN IF SOMEONE IS SAYING WHAT YOU WANT TO HEAR MAKE SURE IT'S WHAT YOU SHOULD HEAR, FROM YOUR HEART.

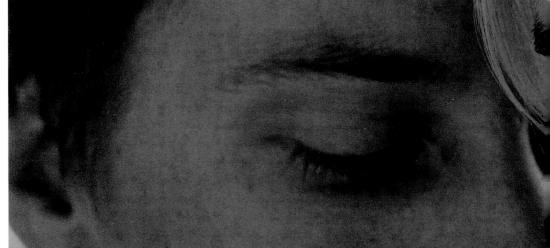

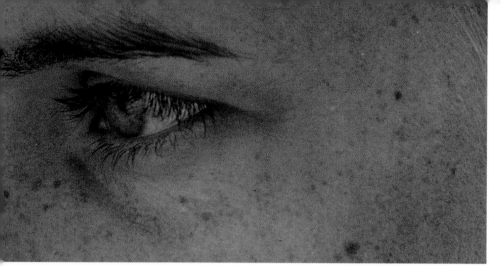

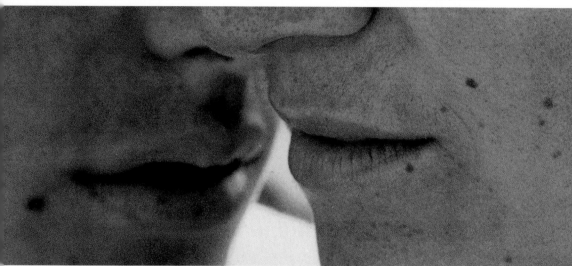

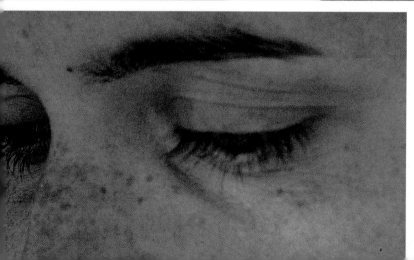

sunrise...sunset

Wake up — time to break up!

It happens sometimes. You go to sleep one night and the next morning when you wake up you can feel that something has definitely, radically changed. You have. And so has your heart. You know that this change will have some far-reaching effects and there will be other changes, too. For starters, your bedroom needs to be redecorated or painted. Next, your boss needs a reality check (your notice on his desk). Then, to wrap things up, your current partner needs to be told: that they're about to become your ex.

There's no way around it. You think you've been kind by engaging in avoidance tactics and FPD (friendly, polite, distant) communication but the reality is your vibe has been giving things away and now it's time to do the right thing. You have to tell them. When the energy changes in a situation — especially in a relationship — you can always feel it. Even if it is painful to acknowledge, don't ignore it. Honor it.

Face up to it and to them. Honestly, simply and without too many excuses. It's a bit like removing a bandage strip — it's usually less painful if you do it quickly and cleanly. If you don't, you're not being honest and your partner is left continuing to believe in something that's no longer true. And that's not fair, to anyone.

Remember, the Universe is watching. Do the right thing. Be kind.

'Tears are a gift
from God. Tears are
for memory, for without
them how could we
remember ourselves?'

|From *Hideous Kinky*,
a film by Charles
MacKinnon

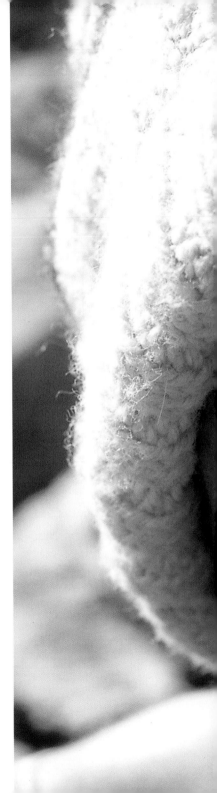

If you must put it in writing

'Dear John' letters may seem like a good idea at the time. 'Why not?' you may think. 'I've got all this anger and hurt inside me and they've treated me badly and I've got to let them know how I feel and how dare they . . .'
But writing down all of your deepest hurts and thoughts and sending them to someone is never really a good idea. Because instead of ending your pain, you will just perpetuate it. If you do need to release your negativity onto a page, write it down then burn it or destroy it.
So instead of writing, simply say what you need to say (calmly, if you can). And then get on with your life. That's the best way to achieve closure.

Trust the one who hesitates and thinks
before they deliver their response.

Love is silent. More often than not.

Sometimes when you win, you really lose. Winning an argument isn't much fun, because you're in a jousting session where everyone's a loser. Opinions are opinions and they have equal weight. Agree to just see things differently. No fight. No winners. No losers.

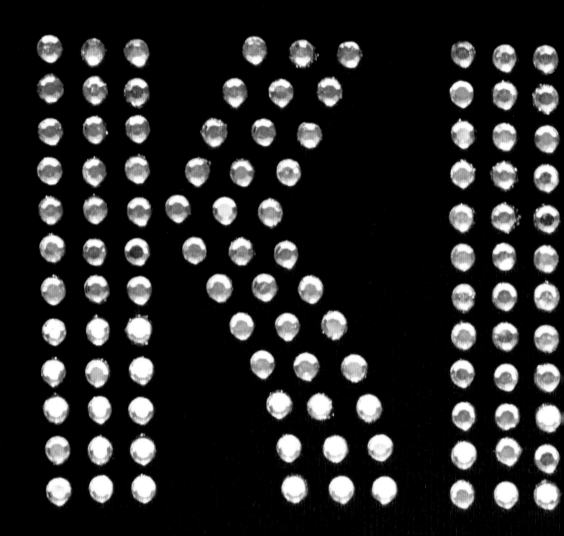

'Love kills you in the ring.'

Girlfight, a film by Karyn Kusama

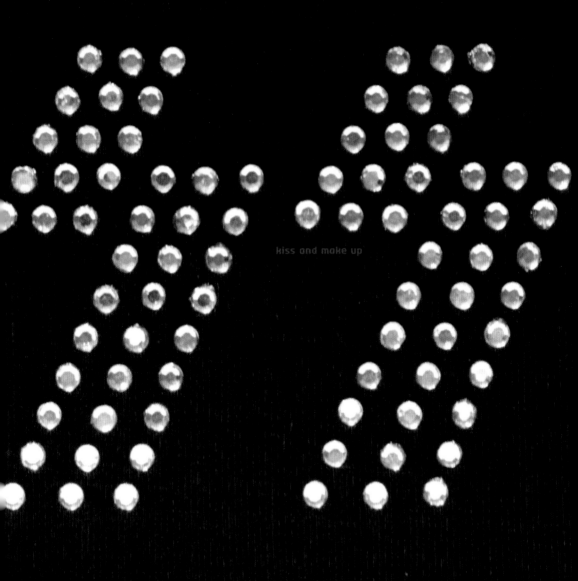

kiss and make up

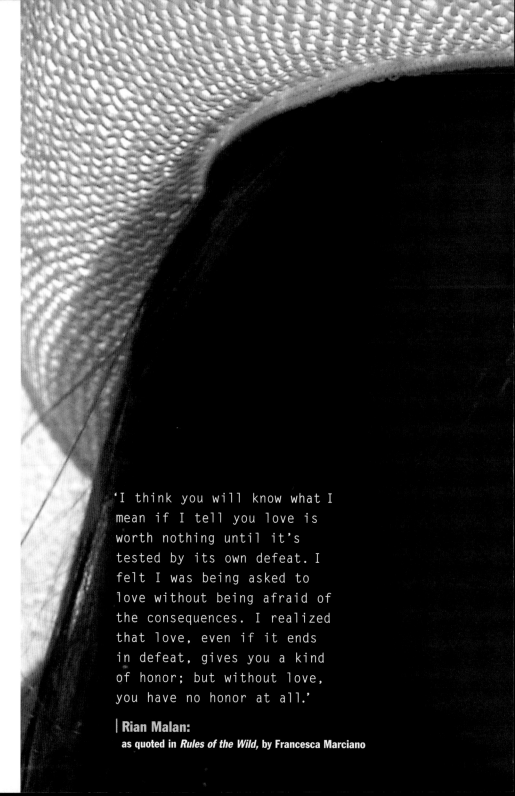

'I think you will know what I
mean if I tell you love is
worth nothing until it's
tested by its own defeat. I
felt I was being asked to
love without being afraid of
the consequences. I realized
that love, even if it ends
in defeat, gives you a kind
of honor; but without love,
you have no honor at all.'

| **Rian Malan:**
as quoted in *Rules of the Wild,* by Francesca Marciano

LOVE is a conversation without end which leads
to the silence of eternity. Love is immortal.

perception

personal
effort
rewards
connection
energy
passing
transforms
individual
outer
need

CHAKRA: **third-eye chakra**: recognition of the metaphysical aspect of 'being' and the connection of the individual to creation; the infinite spiritual intelligence passes through this chakra and by doing so affects and influences the individual as a whole

[def.n] The power or faculty of cognition of a thing or situation; an immediate or intuitive recognition, as of a moral or aesthetic quality or an understanding; a receiving of meaning; the awareness of a fact or of the reality of a situation, person, place or object; being open to understanding; to break through.

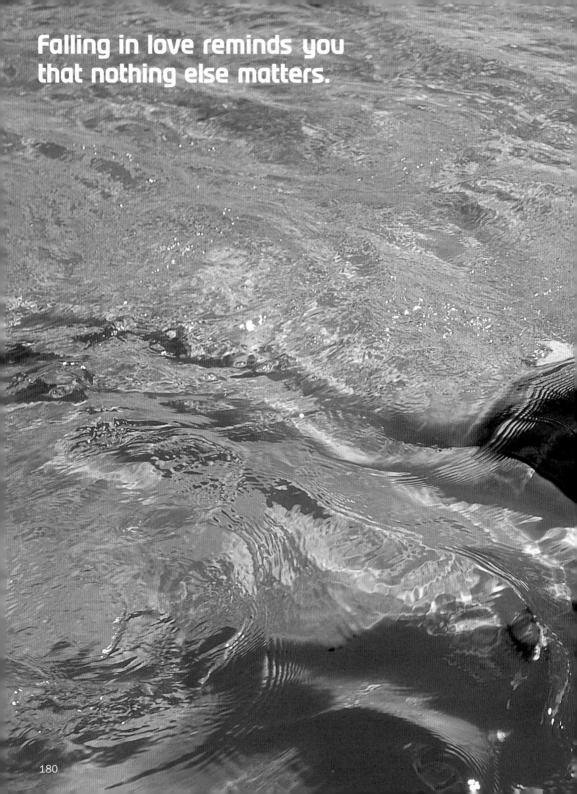

Falling in love reminds you that nothing else matters.

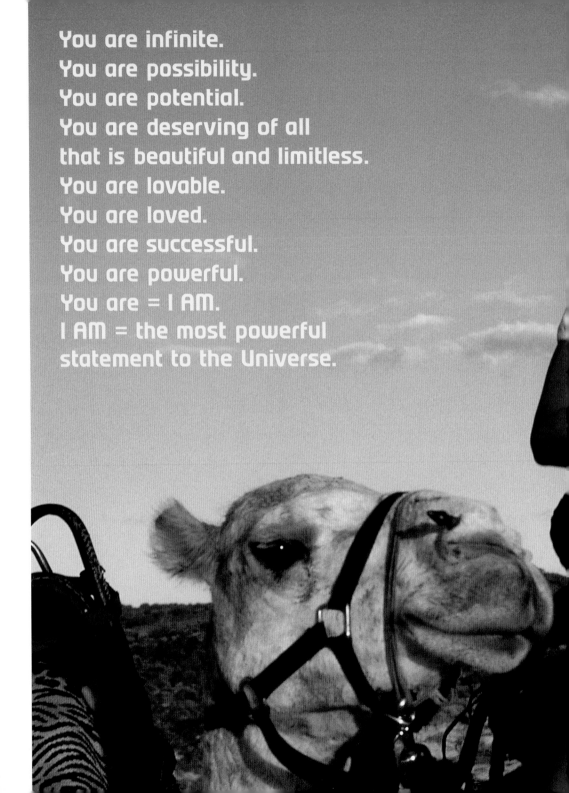

You are infinite.
You are possibility.
You are potential.
You are deserving of all
that is beautiful and limitless.
You are lovable.
You are loved.
You are successful.
You are powerful.
You are = I AM.
I AM = the most powerful
statement to the Universe.

Take hold of your essence.
Center yourself and consolidate
who you are. You. As Yourself.
Not as a being trying to graft
onto another so you both need
to cling to each other, all the
while holding each other back
— or down. Just as a being.
Just a being. Just being. See the
opportunities ahead of you, a
being filled with limitless love and
potential. Fulfil your destiny and
live up to the very best version
of yourself. Your highest Self.

'ALL LOVE IS BASED ON THE

Deepak Chopra, *The Path to Love*

Free love
Whomever you love
let them be free
free to be themselves
free to go
to fulfil their
personal destiny
free to experiment
free to change
free to make mistakes
free to love others
free to be real
free to just be
as you are
free.

It's not easy being green

Welcome to your very own personal demon — envy. Envy is a huge test for almost everyone — male or female - and it is the one thing that is guaranteed to bring even the most secure, stable or accomplished person undone.

So what is envy and where does it come from? Envy is fear. When we are envious of someone — perhaps of what they have, or what they have done — we are affirming to the Universe that we believe there is a lack in ourselves and in the cosmos. And that is pure fear.

To overthrow envy, we have to believe in abundance instead. There's no reason why we should feel angry or upset that someone else has something we would like for ourselves. We all need to see it in terms of what that person's destiny requires for them at this time.

So stop competing and just enjoy being a part of the carnival. There will always be another person who appears to have or be more than you, but this is part of the illusion. It's nowhere near reality. And would you honestly be better off if they didn't have more?

Be happy for someone else to be gorgeous or to have a great boyfriend or a new car. Want the best for everyone and know that you can have the best too. Seeing things this way says much about you as a person - you are both generous and balanced. It's also a flag to the Universe that you're deserving and you're happy to wait your turn, which will come with the right attitude and the right thinking.

There is plenty to go around. Remember that nothing is permanent and time can change everything, for better or worse.

the
face of
love is
kind

LOVE OBJECTS TO LOVE OBJECTS

Nothing is permanent. The words LOVE OBJECT remind us of a type of love that's aesthetic. It's surface deep and can never survive the scrutiny of time, which can only reveal its limitations. Being someone else's love 'object' means being treated as less than who you really are. And that's not love. Be substantial in the first place by refusing to be mere decoration, and be on the lookout for those who wish to make you one.

Model of the year

You are not the same person you were last year, last month or even yesterday. Whatever has gone has gone, and whatever has stayed with you is there for a purpose. Unlike the human body which shows the cracks and signs of wear and tear, love becomes more polished, shinier, and seamless. Love is ageless. And since you came from love it means that you are too. And you're in the 21st century now.

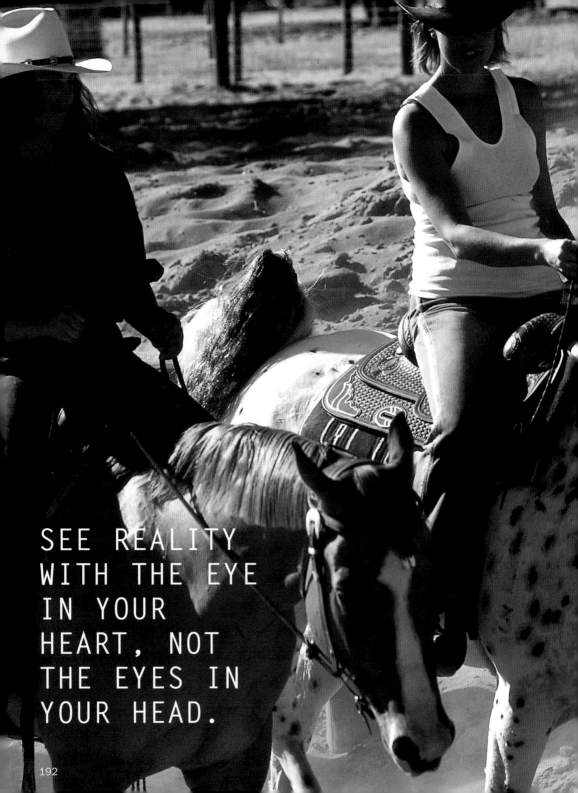

SEE REALITY
WITH THE EYE
IN YOUR
HEART, NOT
THE EYES IN
YOUR HEAD.

THE PATH OF LOVE

RECOGNIZE OTHERS WHO ARE ON YOUR PATH FOR THEY ARE ON THEIRS, TOO, AND YOUR PATHS HAVE CROSSED. BE ALIVE TO THE POSSIBILITY THAT EVERYONE YOU MEET HAS A LESSON FOR YOU AND EVERYONE YOU DEAL WITH MAY BE YOUR TEACHER. THEY MAY TEACH YOU, THROUGH YOUR OWN ACTIONS AND REACTIONS, ABOUT THE OBSTACLES WITHIN YOURSELF, OR HOW YOU NEED TO BE, OR EXACTLY WHERE YOU NEED TO FOCUS AND WORK. LOVE IS A RELEASE THAT RESULTS IN A POSITIVE ENERGY EXCHANGE BETWEEN PEOPLE.

"I've been waiting a long time would send me someone

Sata, Rasta, Negril, Jamaica

Soul mate

When you meet a person you are destined for, there is a knowing that transcends all of the small and unimportant details of living. The person may be a soul mate for life or they may be a soul mate for only part of your journey. All soul connections that you make in your lifetime will register with you energetically. You alone can tell the difference between someone who clocks in at 5.2 or at 9.6 on your personal internal Richter scale. The energy that you feel will alert you to how significant they are going to be for you. It all depends on who you are and where you find yourself. But you will know on a deep level, beyond reason, the connection. A soul mate is one who makes you think and feel in a new way – one who opens up your soul.

When you think your soul mate has passed you by

Maybe you met someone who was your soul mate, but circumstances kept you from being together at the time. If that person is part of your destiny, they will come back into your life at some point in the future. Perhaps they had other lessons to learn in order to be ready for what the two of you are going to experience. Or maybe you needed to be in a different situation or headspace to be able to come together with your soul mate. When and if the time is right – for each of you – you'll meet again.

194

now but I knew Jah [God]
when my time was right.'

'Knowing love, I will allow all things to come and go, to be as supple as
the wind and to take everything that comes with great courage. As Rasa
would say: "Life is right, in any case." My heart is as open as the sky.'

From *Kama Sutra*: a film by Mira Nair

Village girls, Auroville, India

Material girls

For many, materialism is the new spiritualism. The race is on as people all over the world load up with designer accessories, cars, houses – and spouses. Financial extrvagance is encouraged by social pressure and advertising messages that tell us that if we loved our partners or family we'd buy them more stuff. It's a dangerous road to go down and often results in relationships being sacrificed on the altar of consumerism. Wanting more is completely fruitless if you don't appreciate how rich you already are. Focus on the real value in your personal connections and revere them. Goods and services are no substitute. Remember that love cannot be bought, it cannot be produced on demand and it is as priceless as it is free. The really valuable things in life always are.

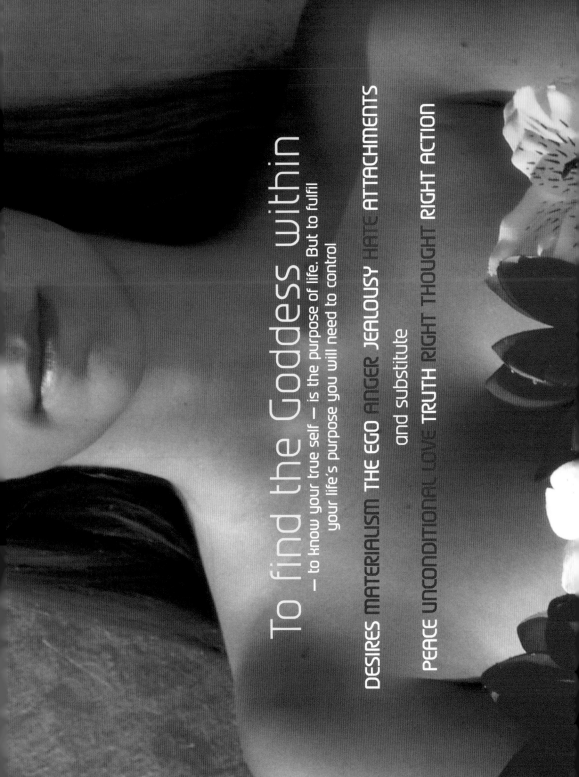

To find the Goddess within

— to know your true self — is the purpose of life. But to fulfil
your life's purpose you will need to control

DESIRES MATERIALISM THE EGO ANGER JEALOUSY HATE ATTACHMENTS

and substitute

PEACE UNCONDITIONAL LOVE TRUTH RIGHT THOUGHT RIGHT ACTION

The ultimate
act of love is
to want the best
for someone in
the highest,
purest way.

watch for
the unguarded
moment

unity

undivided

never

interrupted

trust

yourself

CHAKRA: crown chakra: absolute and total connection with the Universe, the limitations of the self are overcome by the merging of cosmic energies with the pure consciousness of the Divine [def:n] The state or fact of being one; oneness; something complete in itself; the oneness of a complex or organic whole; of interconnectedness; total harmony and fluidity; freedom from diversity or variety; oneness of mind, feeling, body, spirit.

There is no distance

between two hearts

Love story

How we believe in love stories is critical to our own experiences in love. Do you believe it's possible to love another person and that it's not always going to end in tears? Do you believe in happy endings? Or do you believe that loving will inevitably end in sadness or regret? The best love story is not necessarily one of high passion and short burnout. It may be one of longevity and a sense of mutual respect and intimacy, individual growth and sustained combined energy. It may be a relationship that lasts until it becomes a deep friendship, where each individual continues to grow and yet still wants to aim for something higher together. This kind of relationship sustains romance and companionship. It is the result when two people stay together because they want to. The best love story is one that lives and breathes in the present, charting the map of two human hearts, beating as one. The best love story is the one you write together, where you tell your own tales and sing your own songs in the privacy of a world you build together. Identify with the love story that hasn't yet been written. Your love story.

Love is inclusionary, not exclusionary.
Love does not discriminate.
LOVE IS ACCESS ALL AREAS.

211

Take heart
— and follow it

You need to be a little bit hard on yourself when you think you're 'in love' and that this time it's going to be 'The Relationship'. So before you get too involved, ask yourself: Is this person ready? Mature? Right for me? Stable? Secure with whom they are? Do they know what they want? Do they know what I want? Are they willing to commit? Able to stand back and check out the situation as fully as possible and with as much objectivity as you can muster. But always approach it from your heart. Does it feel right? In matters of love, timing is everything. If you think your partner has most things in place, proceed with caution. If you don't accept that the relationship is okay for the time being, but unless the above criteria can be filled at some point in the near future you will probably end up parting.

Do your homework at the start and you'll be prepared for whatever happens. But also remember this: you can rarely see ahead to who or what will come or go from your life. In the end, all you can do is take heart — and follow it.

"

'It is not enough to have more or even to know more, but to live more, and if we want to live more we must love more. Love is "the treasure hid in a field," and this field is our own soul. Here the treasure is found for which the wise merchant "went and sold all he had". And contrary to the law of matter where to give more means to have less, in the law of love the more one gives, the more one has.'

Juan Mascaro, Introduction to *The Bhagavad Gita*

Giving: it's a question of balance

The balance of giving in any relationship is always in a state of flux. It may be 40–60, 60–40, 80–20 or even 10–90 at any particular moment. It's rarely (if ever) a 50–50 thing. Perfect balance may be achieved momentarily, but it depends on both the capacity of each person and the ebb and flow of the relationship.

Expecting exactly 50–50 – a perfectly equal relationship flow at all times – is simply unrealistic. And expectations and obligations kill relationships. So when judging your own relationship ebb and flow, remember how ch'i energy or yin and yang work: the flow is never exactly the same and yet there is always balance and harmony.

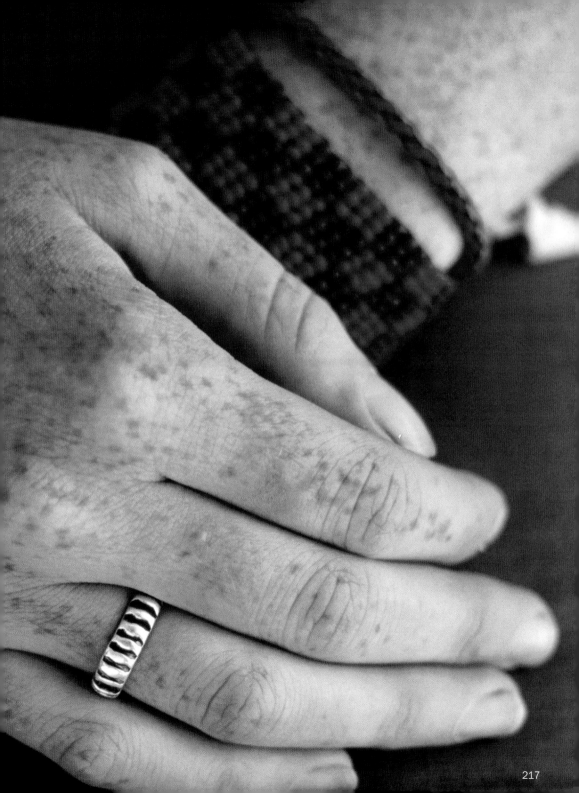

The 'no camping' rule

Once again you find yourself asking 'Your place or mine?', when it strikes you that you're suddenly tired of the question. Or perhaps both of you are feeling that the option of moving in together seems like the easiest one.

Now you're in the danger zone. Because while moving in together seems like the easiest thing to do it may not be the best thing to do in the long term for both of you. So look at the big picture. It's no good going camping just for convenience or to save money, because the tent could be pulled down or blown away at a moment's notice.

When women are asked whether or not they expected moving in together to be permanent, most say they thought it would be. If you ask the guys, however, most of them were not so convinced and often they admit to hedging their bets, with a 'let's see how it goes' attitude.

Many couples face the question of whether to move in together. What counts is each person's intention. Both of you need to have the same intention and it needs to be clearly expressed.

So if you're thinking of moving in together, first agree on the terms. Is it just camping, or is it something more permanent?

Indian

WISE WOMEN DO — and they don't regret it

Nepalese

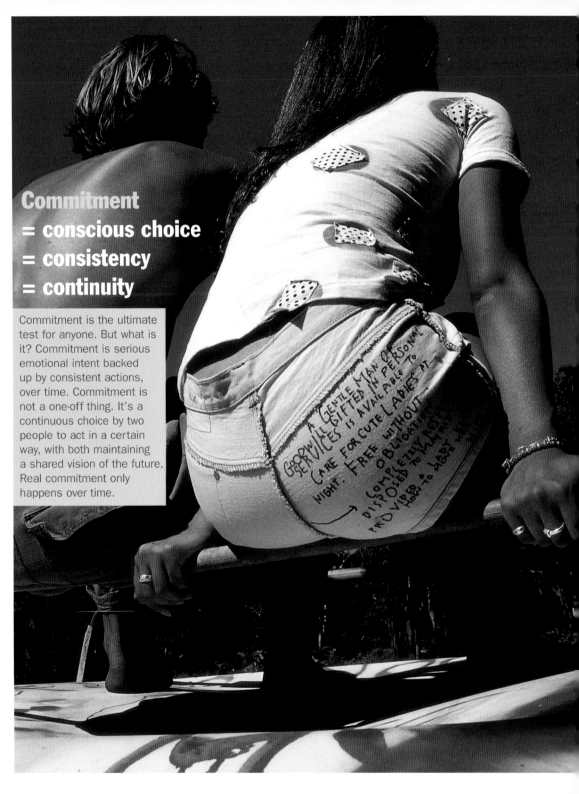

Commitment
= conscious choice
= consistency
= continuity

Commitment is the ultimate test for anyone. But what is it? Commitment is serious emotional intent backed up by consistent actions, over time. Commitment is not a one-off thing. It's a continuous choice by two people to act in a certain way, with both maintaining a shared vision of the future. Real commitment only happens over time.

Stay the course

You must stay your own course, especially when it comes to matters of love. If you have the will and desire and are destined to stay together, nothing will be able to keep you apart.

FREEDOM IS LOVE IN ACTION

LOVE IS NOT ABOUT 'HAVING' OR 'OWNING' SOMEONE. LOVE IS ABOUT 'ALLOWING' A PERSON TO FULFIL THEIR POTENTIAL, AND THAT MEANS BECOMING WELL ACQUAINTED WITH THE NOTION OF FREEDOM AND THE REALITY OF TRUST. GIVING SOMEONE THE FREEDOM TO BE AND TO FULFIL THEMSELVES IS TRULY LOVE IN ACTION. BY EACH PURSUING YOUR OWN MISSION AND ENCOURAGING THE OTHER TO DO THE SAME YOU ARE GIVING EACH OTHER THE FREEDOM TO GROW. BECAUSE THERE IS NO GROWTH WITHOUT FREEDOM. LOVE DOES NOT GROW BEING KEPT ON A LEASH OR IN A BOX. WHEN YOU GRANT FREEDOM, YOU ARE MORE LIKELY TO DEVELOP TRUE INTIMACY, AND THERE IS NO LONGER PRESSURE ON ANYONE TO PROVE THEIR LOVE. BECAUSE YOU ARE PROVING IT ALREADY PURELY BY WANTING THE BEST FOR EACH OTHER. IN THIS ENVIRONMENT, LOVE CAN PROSPER BECAUSE IT'S NOT BASED ON NEEDI- NESS. LOVE BASED ON FREEDOM IS NOT CONDITIONAL — IT IS REAL.

Love charity

Take the emphasis off 'I', 'me' or 'my' and transfer it to others instead. Volunteer with a charity, help those in need, give time to a worthy cause. Send letters, march, raise funds, wear slogans, stand in, send donations, print literature, get signatures — pitch in however you can.

You will elevate your mind to from the personal to the universal and you'll reap the rewards in a global outlook, new people and a bigger heart.

Give from the heart. Not because you have to — but because you want to. And because you can.

Love connects us

Soul mates, twin flames, short-term love affairs, long-term friendships that turn into intimate relationships, long-term intimate relationships that turn into friendships – these are but some of the many forms that love connections take.

Love connections are always real and eternal, no matter how long or little they last. If you believe in past lives, think of them as the continuation of previous connections you have had. All relationships are karmic and each is a stepping stone to your spiritual growth. They are often referred to as sacred contracts between people and as such are all about achieving balance.

Ideally we will each experience many different kinds of love connections, allowing us to be tested in different ways. So remember, spiritual growth is never negative, no matter what goes down in your love connections.

ONE LOVE

I love ♥

just ... happy, i
spent Easter in
Bali !! LOVE YOU HEAPS!
Sammie x

NY NY 10
USA

Jamaica Dec. 1995

VENUS

CRAZON

love Victoria

Edna O'Brien

65c

Fearful Kate bored with her gentle husband in their grey stone house is driven to indiscretions she can hardly handle without Baba's help. But Baba has her own hands full with the passions of her rich and vulgar builder...

Girls in their Married Bliss

love Emma xxx

Congratulations

233

Love child

Some people have a baby to hold their marriage or relationship together. 'Glue babies', as they are sometimes called, do bring couples and families closer together for a time. However, a child will test you, your partner, your relationship and your capacity to love in every way. A baby is never the solution to a problem and it could be the start of a whole lot more. If you're looking for something to keep your relationship together, there's only one 'glue' that really sticks — love.

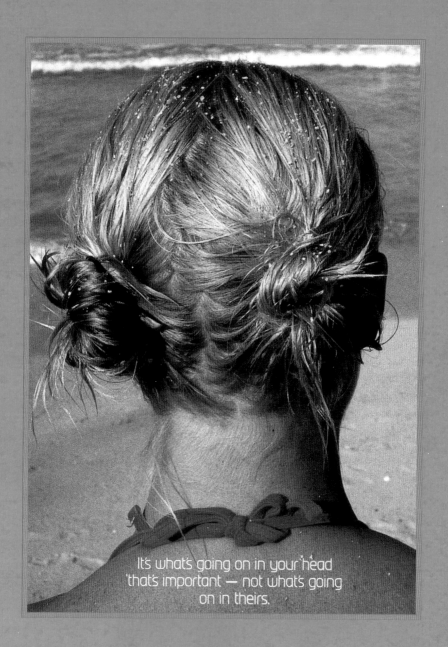

It's what's going on in your head that's important — not what's going on in theirs.

235

Love & marriage

Marriage is simply continuity. It's all about the parallel lives of two people who have the same outlook or vision and have agreed to and are prepared to face it alone, together.

People are often pressured to get married or to be one half of a couple, even when they're not ready or have no need to do so. Being ready for marriage and for real love is a state of mind and a state of being that can only be known by you. No one else can tell you if you're ready for this kind of commitment. Your partner can't tell you; nor can your friends or family. So it's all up to you. You'll know you've taken the first step towards being ready for marriage when you have decided to go on your own personal odyssey: a journey towards self-realization. This is how you gather inner strength and personal resources that lead to honesty, wisdom and a knowledge of self. All these things will make you not only a better communicator but a better person, more confident in your judgment and decisions. You'll be happier too. Single or not. Ready for marriage or not.

Mission church, Kimberley region

Fairytales are people too

People do stay together happily ever after. It really does happen and a lot more often than we think, despite the prevalence of highly publicized break-ups and the gloom and doom divorce statistics. Think positive: for every couple that's splitting up there is another that's staying together. The fairytale ending does exist. Believe it.

Life is eternal
Love is immortal

Sometimes the person you love is taken from you, by distance, another person or even death. Understand that whoever was with you will always be with you. Because even when they take their physical leave of you they leave their love behind. So reject the anger or grief: let it pass over you as a stream over rocks. Hold on to their love instead.

Love can never be destroyed, it can only be let go. Whoever has gone from the earthly plane is now a part of the world around you. All that is pure energy is pure life – and pure love.

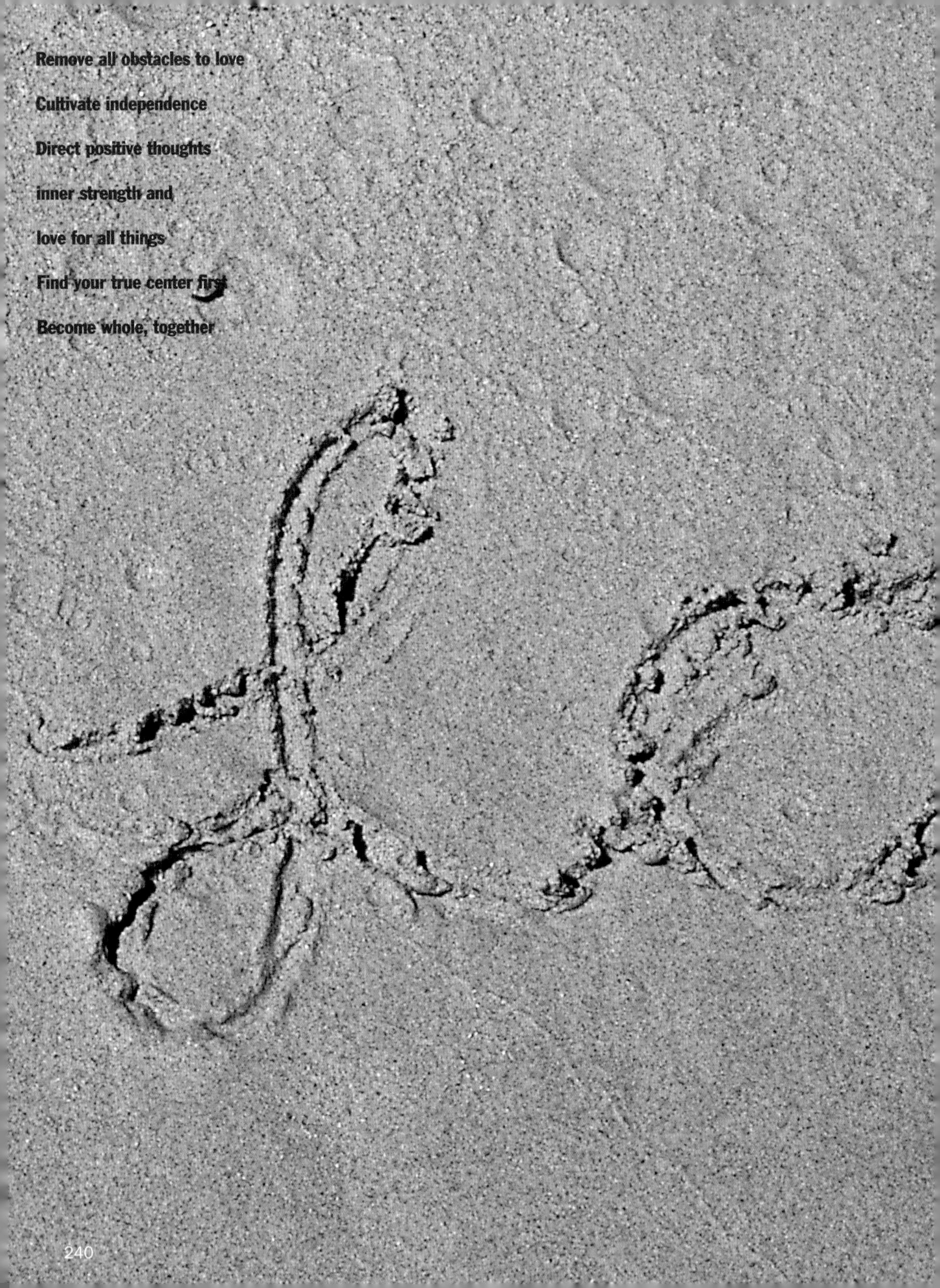

Remove all obstacles to love

Cultivate independence

Direct positive thoughts

inner strength and

love for all things

Find your true center first

Become whole, together

The Girlo crew

Coralee James, 19 [Australia]
Art student, jillaroo
Capricorn
On love 'Love is for the lucky ones – no one wants to be lonely – although freedom is such a strong word and everyone wants to be free.'

Renee Walker, 17 [Australia]
Student, performer
Taurus
On love 'I've learned that I'm always right!'

Kirsty Walker, 15 [Australia]
Student, tapdancer
Cancer
On love 'I don't know about love yet.'

Estelle Azoulay, 24 [France]
Business graduate, traveler
Cancer
On love 'Bring love with you everywhere and sunshine will always surround you.'

Catriona Dowding, 17 [Australia, Yindjibarndi]
Waitress, aspiring photographer
Virgo
On love 'Don't fall hard.'

Jodie Smith, 21 [United Kingdom]
Sales assistant, free spirit
Cancer
On love 'To me love is knowing, security, togetherness, a friend...a soulmate.'

Nikki Ogden, 35 [Australia]
PR & advertising manager, party/surf guru
Virgo
On love 'Love? Oh...I have no idea, oh...I really don't know!'

Crystal Simpson, 15 [Australia]
Surf retail assistant, longboard queen
Gemini
On love 'You can't live without love.'

Sky Anderson, 14 [Australia]
Student, rad surfer, reader
Libra
On love 'Never underestimate the power of love.'

Arna Campbell, 15 [Australia]
Student, rad surfer
Leo
On love 'When you have really strong feelings about someone or something ...it's good to have love in your life.'

Fernanda Ometti, 21 [Brazil]
Hospitality manager, body boarder
Libra
On love 'If you're going to do anything, you've got to be passionate about it. It's all about love!'

Andrew Dowding, 20 [Australia, Ngarluma]
Student, pearl farmer, poet
Libra
On love 'The heart that loves is always young.'

Jasper Dowding, 26 [Australia]
Entrepreneur, freestyle activist, designer
Taurus
On love 'You should maintain balance with honesty and pure intentions.'

Kirri Tranter-Rooke, 18 [Australia]
Medical student, performer
Taurus
On love 'I'm in love right now and I know it's going to last forever.'

Jess Gordon, 16 [Australia]
Student, jazz singer, actor
Sagittarius
On love 'Never refuse an opportunity.'

Sunny & Gypsy Simpson, 12 & 9, Kesta & Dorje Anderson, 12 & 6 [Australia]
Margaret River children
Taurus, Virgo, Taurus, Libra

Steve Creek, 20 [Australia]
Apprentice tradesman, surfer
Virgo
On love 'Love is something you've got to believe in.'

Marissa Boudville, 27 [Australia]
Make-up artist, mother
Taurus
On love 'Hold nothing back and be completely honest.'

Elenni McDonald, 26 [Ethiopia]
Waitress, traveler, music student
Capricorn
On love 'I think love is like a universal language: it doesn't say poor or rich, black or white – it just makes people happy.'

Rebecca Hanlon, 26 [Australia]
Production assistant, retail queen
Cancer
On love 'Love rocks!'

Romy Campbell-Hicks, 21 [Australia]
Camel leader, environmental activist
Libra
On love 'Love is the most beautiful thing on earth, but it can destroy you.'

Ciel Coates, 23 [Australia]
Student, traveler
Pisces
On love 'Love is amazingly natural and beautiful and hidden in everything.'

Danielle Micich, 25 [Australia]
Dancer, choreographer, performance artist
Capricorn
On love 'I'm getting married!'

Cadi McCarthy, 25 [Australia]
Dancer, performance artist
Libra
On love 'It's brilliant if you're with the one you're meant to be with, but sometimes love can be dangerous.'

Tracy Simpson, 42 & George Simpson, 50 [Australia]
Fishing family, artists of life
Virgo & Scorpio
On love 'Love is about always surrendering to the greater truth which forces us to go beyond our fears.'

Julie Anderson, 42 [Australia]
Artist, mother
Pisces
On love 'In relation to loving another person, love means loving their destiny.'

Zoe Henderson, 28 [United Kingdom]
Producer, traveler
Sagittarius
On love 'Unrequited sums it up for me at the moment.'

Jasmin Gidjup, 16 [Australia, Nyoongar]
Animal lover, flower child
Aries
On love 'Boys, family, friends, my dog Zac, my cat Raja – it's a really strong feeling between people…happy stuff!'

Ben Single, 20 & Sofie Pike, 22 [Australia]
Painter, fashion designer; magazine editor, music lover
Aquarius & Taurus
On love 'The sound when you open a bottle of lemonade – if one could feel that intial FFFFZZZZZZ, it would be love.'

Indigo Smart, 6 [Australia]
Fairy child, artist
Gemini
On love 'I don't know what love is AND I don't know anything about love!'

Stacy McCullough, 20 [Canada]
World traveler, explorer
Cancer
On love 'Being alone makes you open your eyes and re-evaluate all of your relationships. It gives you more self-respect. I've learned tons of stuff about myself.'

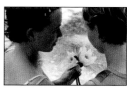

Hayley Preston, 14 [Australia]
Student, skateboarder
Taurus
On love 'You only fall in love once…I guess.'

Girlossary

AURA – the energy emanating from a person, surrounding the body and radiating their moods, character and emotional state. With practise, auras can be seen and they will often present as a particular color or color combination.

BALANCE – a state of equilibrium, calmness and poise; being neutral; mental steadiness and emotional harmony; being in the Universal flow without resistance; being in a state of total acceptance.

CH'I – the essential life force or natural energies of the Universe that are in constant ebb and flow.

CHAKRA – a Sanskrit word meaning 'Wheel of Light'. Sometimes referred to as 'gateways to consciousness', chakras are also known as energy centers within the etheric body that are in constant rotation. Traditionally, there are seven chakras: crown, third eye, throat, heart, solar plexus, lower abdomen and base or root. Each chakra is associated with a specific region of the body, and each has its own purpose and is a source for healing therapy. When chakras are out of balance, healing is required. Rebalancing chakras restores vitality as well as unity to the chakras' combined functioning. Mantras and tones as well as massage can be applied to each chakra for healing. Ultimately, having and maintaining the chakras in balance means that the individual soul can be united (or reunited) with the Collective Universal Soul.

COMMITMENT – an emotional intention backed up by action; a pledge to entrust and which is binding.

COMPASSION – understanding another person's perspective; feeling with and for them, from their point of view, all of their sorrows; having both empathy and sympathy in spirit with others.

CONSCIOUSNESS – the state of being aware of one's own existence and total connectedness with all that is contained within the Universe; complete understanding of all that is and all that will be in eternity; to be spiritually enlightened or awake.

FAITH – confidence, love and trust in a person, belief or thing without requiring proof, in addition to the desire to be an instrument of God's redeeming love.

FIDELITY – the continuous act of standing by promise(s) or obligation(s) and duties; the act of remaining emotionally and sexually monogamous in intimate relationships; strict adherence to truth or fact; honesty.

ILLUSION – that which is not real or which creates a false impression of reality. In the Hindu religion illusion is referred to as 'maya', which means the world of sense experience. Love alone escapes this category. The spiritual seeker seeks release in the Wheel of Life and his or her individuality – to escape maya or provisional reality – to join the World Soul in the ultimate reality.

KARMA – a Sanskrit word meaning action or deed; the exercise of free will, including any physical or mental action. The law of karma is the moral law of cause and effect that states that each act committed by an individual has an equal and opposite reaction back to the individual. All of our acts or karma throughout our lives result in our individual and collective destiny.

KARMIC RELATIONSHIP – a binding connection with a person with whom, through forgiveness and compassion, we have an opportunity to balance karma, in service of divine love. It may be either lasting or temporary in nature.

LOVE – the source energy of all creation; a feeling of deep regard, fondness, and devotion for; deep affection usually accompanied by yearning or desire for; affection between persons more or less founded on, or combined with, desire or passion;

an unconditional spiritual state of bliss and ecstasy with life.

LOYALTY – faithful to one's oath, promise or obligations; complete and unwavering acceptance and support of a situation, a friend, family member or lover.

MARRIAGE – an intimate and spiritual union between two people that is frequently legal in nature but more and more often a bond based purely on an understanding of commitment, morality and life choices between individuals; an agreement to share karma with another.

MATERIALISM – a philosophical theory that regards physical matter and its motions as constituting the Universe, and which holds that all phenomena (including thought) are the result of material things; the devotion to material rather than spiritual objects, needs and considerations.

PERSISTENCE – to continue steadily on a course of action, purpose or thought; to do something in a lasting or enduring way, especially despite opposition or obstacles.

REINCARNATION – the process by which an individual soul passes through a sequence of bodies, also known as 'transmigration of the soul'. In the Hindu religion the spirit depends on the body only to the same extent that a body depends on the clothes it wears. In the human body, the soul is conscious of itself. Reincarnation of the soul into the human body means that the law of karma applies.

SENSUALITY – in relation to exploration, experience and gratification of the physical senses.

SOUL – the essential eternal being and the blueprint for immortality; the spiritual part of a person or being.

SOUL MATE – a person with whom one has a deep connection at a soul or spiritual level; someone who makes one think and feel in a new way; one who opens up another's soul; a soul that brings out the best in another.

TARA – Tara is a female deity in Buddhism. The name Tara means 'She who liberates': she who protects human beings while they are crossing the ocean of existence (samsara). There are two forms of Tara: Green Tara and White Tara. They hold a very prominent position in the cultures of Tibet and Nepal and represent the positive aspects of women. It is said that in the pain of samsara, two tears fell from the eyes of Avaloketishvara, the Boddhisattva of compassion and were transformed into the two Taras. Green Tara is the manifestation of the wife of King Songsten Gampo of Tibet (5th or 6th century), a princess from Nepal. White Tara is the manifestation of his other wife, a princess of China. These two women are regarded as being the physical manifestation of the two Taras. They are acknowledged for their compassion and for the expansion of Buddhism within Tibet.

TRANSCEND – to rise above, surpass, excel, pass through or be beyond the range, sphere or power (of human understanding, physical experience etc).

TRUST – reliance on the integrity, justice, sense of honour of a person or situation, or on some quality of some attribute or thing; confidence that something will occur; hope.

TWIN FLAME – souls that are created together in the beginning; two halves of a divine whole, male and female polarities, with the same spiritual origin and unique pattern of identity; the highest form of soul mate. Each incarnation spent apart from one's twin flame was either spent creating or balancing the karma that is the only obstacle to reunion. We each have a unique mission with our twin flame, but wholeness within self is the first step.

Thank yous & acknowledgements

THANK YOU . . . Deepest thanks to all those who have participated in and contributed to this project. Your generosity and enthusiasm will always be remembered.

The Universe, Michael and Sandra Paul, Cathy Derksema, Justine O'Donnell, Ashley de Prazer, Marcus Clinton, Lawrence Dowd, Rebecca Hanlon, Beth Sargent, Jude McGee, Sophie Cunningham, Simone Ford, Lou Playfair, Karen Williams, Angela Jonassen, Simone Begg, Kelly Brockhoff, Jessica Adams, Dan Single, Tsubi, Lindy Wylie, Coelho, Hugo Paul, Vianney Johnson, Nikki Ogden, Rusty Surfboards, Tom Middleton, Gemma Dacer, Bianca Polinelli, Sandy Archer, Paul Wilson, Jonathan Zawada and Steve Gorrow of The Revolution, Peter Dowding, Tracy and George Simpson, Julie Anderson, Jasper Dowding, Catriona Dowding, Andrew Dowding, Jess Gordon, Steven Creek, Ciel Coates, Renee Walker, Kirsty Walker, Crystal Simpson, Sky Anderson, Arna Campbell, Fernanda Ometti, Hayley Preston, Kirri Tranter-Rooke, Stacy McCullough, Tim Delaney, Romy Campbell-Hicks, Jasmin Gidjup, Sunny Simpson, Gypsy Simpson, Kesta Anderson, Sanjai and Dorje Anderson, Danielle Micich, Cadi McCarthy, Jodie Smith, Coralee James, Marissa Boudville, Elenni McDonald, Estelle Azoulay, Skye and Hannah Gunning, John Martin, Jackie O'Brien, Miriam Stiel, Jaime Marina, Peter and Kerry Davies, Derek Hynd, Dale Egan, Sally Prisk, Clinton Barnes, Alan Linney, South Sea Pearl Exchange, Zoe Henderson, Sofie Pike, Ben Single, Dariya Gratte and Indigo Smart, Fiona Coogan, Bernadette Wyer, Tim Nott, Jay Davies, Helena Reid, Namgyel Tsering, Joan and Don Wilson, Ghinny and Sam Lau of screen, Tony Dormer, The Tibetan Friendship Group.

And finally, many thanks to WA and especially to Yallingup – 'Place of Love by the Water' . . . the memories will never fade.

Photography

Ashley de Prazer, pages: viii, xiv–1, 4–5, 7–20, 24–7, 42–3, 46–7, 50–1, 53, 56–61, 64–5, 68–75, 78–9, 81, 88, 92, 95, 97–9, 104–7, 112, 114–17, 119, 120–5, 128–31, 134–5, 138, 142–3, 148, 151, 158–63, 167, 169–71, 174–5, 180–5, 187–9, 191–205, 208–9, 212–18, 220–3, 225, 228–9, 234–9.
Marcus Clinton, pages: iv–v, xi, 2–3, 6, 22–3, 28–31, 36–7, 44–5, 63, 76–7, 86–7, 90–1, 93, 110–11, 144–5, 154, 157, 164–5, 172–3, 176–9, 206–7, 220–1, 226–7, 230, 233, 234–5, 240–1.
Lawrence Dowd, pages: 32, 34–5, 40–1, 48–9, 54–5, 66–7, 84–5, 100–2, 108–9, 126–7, 132–3, 140–1, 152–3, 211, 220–1, 248–9.

Film credits

The Cup: Dendy Films and Palm Pictures present *The Cup*, a film by Khyentse Norbu. a Coffee Stain production. released by Dendy Films.
Himalaya: Jacques Perrin, Galatee Films present *Himalaya,* a film by Eric Valli, produced by Jacques Perrin and Christophe Barratier.
Kama Sutra: NDF International Ltd, Pony Canyon Inc., Pandora Films in association with Channel Four Films present a Mirabai Films Production, *Kama Sutra*, a film by Mira Nair.
Girlfight: REP and TRIBE and The Independent Film Channel present a Green/Renzi production, a film by Karyn Kusama, *Girlfight*.
Hideous Kinky: The Film Consortium and BBC Films present in association with The Arts Council of England, a Green Point Film, co–production with AMU, a film by Charles MacKinnon, *Hideous Kinky*.

Favorite books

Here is my personal list of some wonderful and very helpful books that I've come across on my travels. Some of them are timeless classics; others have been published more recently but may well be considered classics in the future. Some are quirky, some humorous, some simply timely. What they each contain, however, is great wisdom on love, life and relationships. All have served at one point or another to remind me that my quest is not solitary and that there are many fellow seekers on the same road.

A book can be a catalyst for personal change, insight and awareness, all of which I hope and believe these references will bring you in abundance, as well as peace, joy, love and light on your journey.

Jessica Adams, *The New Astrology for Women*, HarperCollins Publishers Australia, Sydney, 1998.

Deepak Chopra, *The Path to Love*, Rider Books, Random House, London, 1997.

Paulo Coelho, *The Alchemist*, HarperPerennial, HarperCollins Publishers, San Francisco, 1994.

Jonathan Cott, *The Search for Omm Sety*, Warner Books, New York, 1987.

H H The Dalai Lama, Freedom in Exile: T*he Autobiography of the Dalai Lama of Tibet*, Sphere Books, Cardinal, United Kingdom, 1991.

Stephanie Dowrick, *The Universal Heart*, Viking, Penguin Books, Melbourne, 2000.

Kahlil Gibran, *The Prophet*, Penguin Books, London, 1992.

Harville Hendrix, *Keeping the Love You Find*, Pocket Books, Simon & Schuster, New York, 1992.

Anne Morrow Lindbergh, *Gift from the Sea*, Pantheon Books, Random House Inc., New York, 1955, 1997 edition.

Francesca Marciano, *Rules of the Wild*, Vintage Books, Random House, New York, 1998.

Juan Mascaro (trans.), *The Bhagavad Gita*, Penguin Books, London, 1962.

Toni Morrison, *Tar Baby*, Signet, Penguin Books, New York, 1983.

Elizabeth Clare Prophet, *Soul Mates and Twin Flames*, Summit University Press, Gardiner, United States, 1999.

Karen Salmansohn, *Even God is Single*, Workman Publishing Co. Inc., New York, 2000.

Andy Warhol, *Love, Love, Love*, Bullfinch Press, Little Brown & Co. (Canada) Ltd, Toronto, 1995.

Marianne Williamson, *A Return to Love*, HarperCollins Publishers, New York, 1992.

Marianne Williamson, *A Woman's Worth*, Random House, New York, 1993.

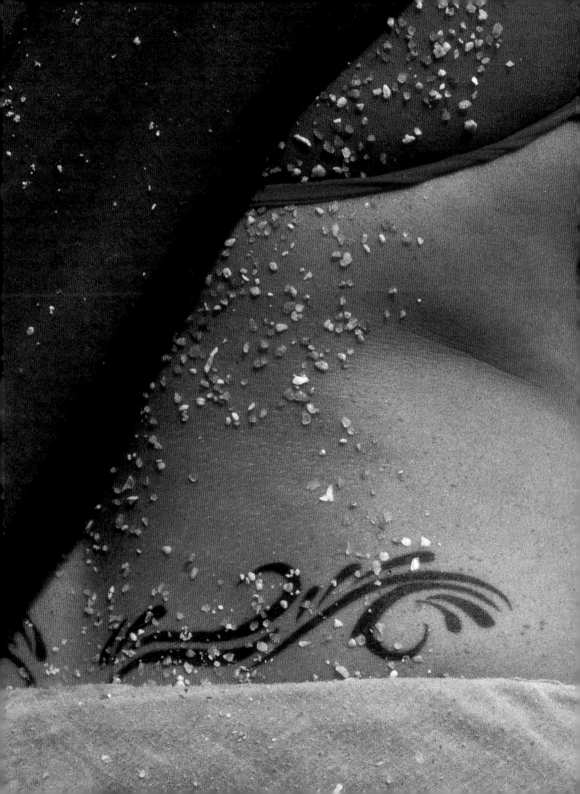

'Perhaps this is the most important thing for me to take back from beach-living: simply the memory that each cycle of the tide is valid; each cycle of the wave is valid; each cycle of a relationship is valid. And my shells? I can sweep them all into my pocket. They are only there to remind me that the sea recedes and returns eternally ... The waves echo behind me. Patience — Faith — Openness is what the sea has to teach. Simplicity — Solitude — Intermittency ...but there are other beaches to explore. There are more shells to find. This is only a beginning.'

Anne Morrow Lindbergh, *Gift from the Sea*

each of us to our personal destiny